Praise

Let Them Speak!

"It's time for every educator to do what we're asking our students to do on a daily basis: embrace feedback and then make changes that benefit our students. Coda and Jetter have done a fantastic job of showing how our students have valuable opinions that are just waiting to be shared—opinions that could unlock the secrets to even more success in our classrooms and schools. We have to actively make the choice to take student feedback seriously and analyze it in order to make improvements in everything that we do. And who knows our teaching better than our own students?"

—**Paul Solarz,** Grade 5 teacher and author of *Learn Like a PIRATE*

"*Let Them Speak!* will truly transform your mind as an educator! After reading this book, you will want to ask your students the important questions, and once you DO start asking them the important questions, student voice will break open the blood clot of the status quo and enable the blood to flow and be restored in your school!"

—**Isaiah Sterling,** Grade 11 student and moderator of #weleadby

"If your goal is to transform your classroom, school, or district and provide a true student-focused learning experience, you will want to read *Let Them Speak!* and take action. That goes for state education leaders too!"

—**Johnny Key,** commissioner, Arkansas Department of Education

"Powerful, provocative, and positive. This quick and easy read is filled with student stories that will move you to action. The authors convinced me that the path to lasting and meaningful school transformation is to simply let them speak!"

—**Kimberli Breen,** national MTSS consultant, school psychologist, and school improvement trainer

"*Let Them Speak!* is a breath of fresh air in so many aspects, and educators everywhere will be able to relate, innovate, and move forward with the ideas expressed by Coda and Jetter. Student voice is so absolutely important, and actually following through with asking kids about their interests is something we all need to be doing more of in our schools. *Let Them Speak!* will leave you energized and ready to tackle any new idea or project you have, so go get after it now, and let them speak!"

—**Adam Welcome,** award-winning principal, director of innovation, author, and cofounder of *Kids Deserve It!*

"Achieving impactful student involvement in schools requires a thoughtful and reflective understanding of why student voice is so important. Every educator should read *Let Them Speak!* in order to gain insight into the need for student input and to share the book with their school teams."

—**Dr. Angel Jannasch-Pennell**, CEO and cofounder, KOI Education

"Coda and Jetter remind us that student voice is not only a transformational initiative but a second-order cultural change for schools. As we continue to strive for school improvement, we must discontinue 'doing school to students' and begin bringing the students to the table in collaborative efforts. It is the students' table, anyway! With a focus on external transformation standards, assessments, and accountability, we often neglect the most important piece of the process: input from our students. This internal transformation not only changes the learning culture, but Coda and Jetter remind us that student voice makes a positive impact on student motivation and student learning. If you are an educator looking for an internal transformation, *Let Them Speak!* is for you."

—**Dr. Blaine Alexander**, program leader: school support and organizational development, Arkansas Leadership Academy

"If you are looking for meaningful student involvement and effective ways to get educator buy-in to the process, *Let Them Speak!* is a must-read. It's a detailed examination into the importance of the why and how of including student voice in any school setting."

—**Karen Gifford,** director of strategic initiatives, KOI Education

"Imagine a business that ignored its customers. How successful do you think it would be? So why do policymakers predominantly ignore student input when it comes to improving schools? Coda and Jetter should be commended for creating a book that is long overdue. Anyone interested in improving education needs to read this magnificent *Let Them Speak!* manifesto."

—**Dr. Danny Brassell**, CalStateTEACH faculty advisor, internationally acclaimed education speaker, and author of *Bringing Joy Back into the Classroom*

"I feel good when my teachers care for me. I like it when I feel like they are on my side. It helps me to be able to tell them all of my feelings. Everyone should have teachers like this, and that's what this book can help with."

—**Ellen Jetter,** Grade 4 (Yes, this is Rick's daughter.)

"Maybe this book will help to stop things from going on and on and on—things that might upset or hurt kids even if teachers don't really mean to hurt kids. It's important for us to share our stories and speak up so we feel better each day about going to school. I like when my teachers care about what I think. Sometimes I think I have some really good ideas too."

—**Nora Jetter,** Grade 6 (Yes, this is Rick's other daughter.)

"My dad and his friend wrote *Let Them Speak!* to help kids. I think that teachers should talk to kids about how to make school more fun for them while they are learning. If the teachers and staff were in our shoes, they wouldn't want school to be boring, either. They would want it to be something they are looking forward to each morning and even wake up early for!"

—Eddie Jetter, Grade 8 (Yes, this is Rick's son.)

Rebecca Coda & Rick Jetter

HOW STUDENT VOICE
CAN TRANSFORM
YOUR SCHOOL

Let Them Speak!

© 2018 by Rebecca Coda and Rick Jetter

This book is available at special discounts when purchased in quantity for use as premiums, promotions, fundraisers, or for educational use. For inquiries and details, contact the publisher at books@daveburgessconsulting.com.

Published by Dave Burgess Consulting, Inc.
San Diego, CA
daveburgessconsulting.com

Cover Design by Genesis Kohler
Editing and Interior Design by My Writers' Connection

Library of Congress Control Number: 2018933913
Paperback ISBN: 978-1-946444-67-7
eBook ISBN: 978-1-946444-68-4
First Printing: April 2018

Dedication

Let Them Speak! is *about* students and *for* students.

It will help educators and parents to realize that changing the landscape of education relies on activating student voice.

Our hope is that adult egos can be set aside so that listening to our students becomes the number one initiative for reforming education. Student voices are the most expert opinions anyone could get.

This one is for students everywhere because we know you are counting on us!

CONTENTS

Serendipity

A foreword written by the following:

Christina Vail, master teacher;
Grace Ghali, Karissa Wade, and Sal Shoban,
master students and STEAM girls from
Hamilton High School, Chandler, Arizona

It is the supreme art of the teacher to awaken joy in creative expression and knowledge.

—Albert Einstein

Have you ever caught yourself in a moment of time, and you knew that you were in that space and time for a reason? The happenstances were unexplainable, yet they felt undeniably purposeful? The events that connected us to this manuscript are one of those "serendipitous moments," and we are elated to tell our story.

I have always been known as a strong, hardworking, thoughtful, high school drama teacher. I identify, first, as a mother raising my own children. I also possess difference-making qualities in my life when working with and for others. This, especially, applies to being an educator. My life is dedicated to making a difference in the life of each and every student who passes through my classroom door. Every student, no matter their background, will succeed in my classroom. They just *will*. Every student matters.

As the 2016–2017 school year began, a class that I had been teaching since 2001—known as "Stagecraft"—was renamed and realigned in the high school course catalog, morphing into a career and technical education (CTE) course now called "Technical Theatre." It requires a STEAM focus. The change from "Stagecraft" to "Technical Theatre" also required increased academic rigor, increased funding from the state, and population tracking mandated by our new state requirements. As the student rosters were formed and the new year started, we began tracking all of the necessary data for analyzing our program. One of the required data points that needed to be tracked was the pattern and ratio of gender success within the course. My eyes opened wide when I looked at the class data to discover that there was something unusual going on with our female population of "nontraditional" students. Unlike the majority of Technical Theatre programs, our program had a male-to-female ratio almost opposite of any other in our school and perhaps across the state as well.

Like many educators, I thrive on collaborating with colleagues, friends, and meeting new educational connections. One evening, I was out at dinner with a group of educator friends just catching up with each other. Over the course of the meal I was asked how the school year was going, so I shared my unusual finding of this male-to-female ratio phenomenon of the nontraditional CTE course that I was teaching. I was excited to share that our female nontraditional students were nearly double the enrollment to that of the males. This was important to me because it was a point of hope for our future female leaders regarding participation in STEAM programs.

One of the dinner attendees was Dr. Angel Jannasch-Pennell, the CEO and research director of KOI Education, and she had been intently listening to me share my findings while we dined together. Dr. Jannasch-Pennell also happened to be an organizer for the annual Behavioral Education Technology Conference (BET-C) held in Phoenix each year. She believed that my work and findings, all bundled up in such an amazing story, would be such a powerful addition to the conference, so she asked me if I would do a presentation on how to increase female participation in STEAM classes. Eager to please my friend (and conference organizer), I immediately said "yes"—but then I had a problem. I really had no idea why our STEAM program was attracting more females than males. I was just as curious as my colleagues as to why so many females were enrolling in my STEAM-related course. So I decided to do something novel: I would talk to my students to get answers. I would simply just ask them! I would intentionally Let Them Speak!

The next day I went to school with a mission. I was going to pick my students' brains and find out what the magic ingredients were because I was dying to know. I sat down with my current group of females in my second-period Technical Theatre class. I shared our current statistics with the girls and asked them why they thought so many females were enrolled in my CTE STEAM program course. I was both delighted with the depth of their answers and heartbroken by some of the comments they shared with me.

Their stories were so profound that I knew I couldn't present at BET-C alone; I had to bring these students and empower *them* to tell *their* story. It was apparent to me that I was not qualified to speak about why our program had attracted more female students. It was the students' story to tell.

Fast-forward to the BET-C. While presenting with my amazing female students, Rebecca Coda was sitting in the audience and became captivated by the passion and conviction of my high school STEAM girls. Out of the corner of my eye, I could see that Rebecca had grabbed her cell phone and was intently texting someone. Later I found out that she had texted Dr. Rick Jetter, who was tending to their Pushing Boundaries Consulting booth and exhibit in the lobby before they were scheduled to present and told him to get down to our room ASAP to listen to what my STEAM girls had to say about the power of student voice.

After the presentation, Rebecca and Rick talked to us for quite some time about a book that they were writing about student voice and reassured me that the success of our program was the *outcome* of student voice. The power of my program hinged on me asking my students for insights. If you had told me to do that in the past, I might have responded positively, but now more than ever, I am convinced that our students have the answers. And my STEAM girls were right. Their insights were brilliant. All I did was ask my students what they thought, and the responses that I received were more powerful than I could have ever imagined.

Meeting Rick and Rebecca at the BET-C was more than seren-dipity. It was the moment when all my years of teaching, the events that had occurred with CTE programming, and the power of these passionate students all collided for amazing reasons. My students of Technical Theatre are more than students; they are ambassadors of equity, empowerment, and belonging. Their only intention was to be heard so that all educators would be inspired to listen to them and make an even bigger impact on even more students for years to come.

Because of this series of events and the fact that we place student voice at the forefront of our own work, Rebecca and Rick invited all of us to write this collaborative foreword. The power of our presen-tation at the BET-C rested on my students, just as it will frame the power and set the stage for this book.

Student empowerment is not about teacher domination of the classroom; it is about guiding students, but still allowing them to learn and grow on their own.

—Grace Ghali

What Grace Ghali Has to Say

If you were to ask my friends and family about me, they would describe me as captivating, outgoing, and witty. I love cats and enjoy the solitude and comfort of rainy weather. I believe that staying true to myself is more important than changing to appease others. This was my message of courage and integrity that I shared while presenting to educators at the BET-C. Mrs. Vail gave me a voice, and I am grateful for that. She brought out the best in me and allowed me to make an impact, not only in my life path, but for sharing new possibilities of journeys for many students to come. I didn't always have a voice, you know.

Back in the seventh and eighth grade, my school had a reading requirement called SSR (silent sustained reading). For about thirty minutes before the end of the school day, every student on campus was required to stop what they were doing and just read for this allotted amount of time. Most people I asked never really enjoyed it. Usually the students wouldn't even read; they would just mess around on their phones or talk to their friends across the room using various arbitrary hand signals. The administrators and teachers, however, never bothered to actually ask the students if it was a rewarding or productive initiative. There certainly wasn't any accountability to monitor the program's success.

While we all know that reading is vitally important, we knew that the program was a waste of time. You'd think the adults would have noticed that it wasn't working. Maybe they knew it wasn't working but didn't want to do anything about it, much less listen to our concerns or insights that would only appear to be the result of laziness or rebellion. Had they bothered to ask us about SSR, maybe we wouldn't have lost ninety hours of instructional time over the course of an entire school year and could have used it to accomplish something amazing!

Let Them Speak! points out that administrators and teachers can transform their schools in the right direction: toward us! One part of the book that stands out to me (especially when thinking about my days in junior high) is that "Sometimes what we think is an awesome philosophy, lesson, or policy that pleases them (the adults who create something) might not be anything that helps us (the students receiving the products created by adults) to actually learn better or care about our learning." I thought that this portion of the book, with such a bold statement and concept, was insightful because it rings true for me and many other students that I have met over my years of attending school. Teachers and school leaders sometimes almost never stop to think about how the students may feel about a decision being made—even though most decisions are said to be made with the (supposed) well-being of the students in mind.

I believe this book gives great insights into the minds of students and how their involvement with their own education can create a better environment, not only for them, but also for the very same teachers and administrators who make most of the decisions about our schooling on a daily basis. The point of a school is not to be a place where students dread going when they wake up in the morning; it's meant to be a place of learning, discovery, excitement, and enrichment. So, how can we reach these goals without considering the viewpoints of the students who are doing (or would like to do) such things? Requesting communicative feedback from students about the conditions of education will breed a healthier and more dynamic school environment, which is exactly what *Let Them Speak!* so eloquently does.

> ## If you want me to be the best version of me, then walk with me and talk with me, and I will share with you what impacts me the most.
>
> –Karissa Wade

What Karissa Wade Has to Say

Most of the teachers I've had (this does not go for *all* teachers) believe that some of the decisions they make are in the best interests of students. But the reality is that many teacher and administrator decisions frustrate and limit student potential. In my experience as a student, some of my non-elective teachers are quick to dismiss the requirements or suggestions made by elective teachers for the students. I will never forget the time my English teacher lectured me about coming late to class one day (even though I had a late pass) because I was working on a video for the upcoming sports assembly for the school in my film class, which was the period just before English class. My teacher asked me if I felt that my "little videos" were more important than her class. As someone who wants to major in film study in college and who is trying to build my portfolio, this comment made to me by my teacher was beyond frustrating and made me dread going to her class each and every day.

Though my being late to my teacher's class understandably annoyed her teacher, the condescending attitude and refusal to acknowledge that I was working on something important to both me and to the school was what discouraged me from wanting to be a better student in her class. If my teacher had asked me why I was late or how I could support making up any missed work, I would not only have been more invested in English class, I would have helped find a mutual solution based on a respectful relationship that teachers and students can have with one another. But I felt disrespected.

Let Them Speak! addresses the idea that a lot of school faculty only step up when things are going poorly. Educators often forget to acknowledge what's good about a student and miss the fact that students really *do* want to be successful. The intent of the educator may very well be to ensure that every student is doing well and will be successful in life beyond school, but that's not the real problem in schools today. The problem is that it is discouraging when teachers are only ever active in our lives when something is wrong. Student voice is meant to be a proactive measure, not reactive when things go south. This problematic approach in our schools not only makes students feel as though we are failing or doing poorly, it also dismisses all the times that we do succeed and want to speak up about it. And the truth is, I succeeded many times prior to walking into English class a few minutes late.

Celebrating the successes of our media department making videos for the school or taking time to talk to us is an amazing gesture of kindness and students deserve kindness and sensitivity. Taking some time to talk to us (other than when there's a real problem or a perceived problem) can go a long way in making a student feel accomplished and important in school. Student voice matters to us and we just want so badly to be heard!

This book shines a light on a lot of the issues and contradictions in the educational system that can easily be fixed. I believe that when you read *Let Them Speak!*, you can simply apply even just one thing from this book to help your teaching methods or leadership initiatives in order to improve your students' experiences. There are many teachers and school faculty members, just like Mrs. Vail, who understand the concepts presented in this book and lead by example each day. These are the teachers I will always remember and even stay in contact with because they respect students, honor their voices, make all the difference in a child's world, and believe that students' thoughts and insights are important.

It is obvious to me that when a teacher is truly invested in my success, it is because they take the time to ensure that my classroom experiences meet my needs.

–Sal Shoban

What Sal Shoban Has to Say

I am not the type of person who has an easy time describing myself because I just am who I am. Some people have described me as a natural leader, a person who can lead those who need help. I've also been told that I add direction and focus to nearly any group. One thing I can't deny is that I have a fierce and complex intelligence that intertwines with thoughtfulness and understanding. Ever since I was a child, I have been tough. I never cared what other people thought about me; why should I care what someone thinks about me when my opinion is the only one that matters? I speak up on things I believe in, like at the BET-C Conference. I was brave and bold because the only way to change the world is to tell the world the change it needs.

While speaking about female empowerment in the classroom at the BET-C, I met two hysterical authors. Rebecca and Rick approached me and my convicted group of STEAM girls after our first conference presentation, which I will never forget. Their tone was different than many other educators because it was a tone of mutual respect, and they had different perspectives about teaching than I normally encounter in school. I instantly warmed up to them and related to their views on the power of student voice and offering students Disney®-quality customer service that should be the mantra in all schools. They elevated the student as a stakeholder when they spoke and believed student empowerment meant to also help run the class. I appreciated every word they had to say on our students' behalf.

When I was a small child timidly walking through the crowded kindergarten halls, I always felt looked down upon, like the whole world of the adults I was supposed to admire and respect couldn't care much about me. I felt that, to them, I was just another child dripping in naivety that would probably go on to a mediocre life and career with my newly acquired ABCs and 123s that they were going to teach me.

When I got older, I remember giving one of my teachers an answer (which she had asked us for) about how Frankenstein's monster personified the innermost turmoil of humanity that every person struggles through at some point in their life. My teacher proceeded to tell me that my idea "overanalyzed" her question and was not what she had asked for. Yet, when her teacher aide agreed with me and defended my insights about the book, my teacher went along with her own elaboration on my original idea without even crediting me or apologizing to me for insulting me in front of the whole class. It's attitudes like this which cause children to want to shut down and not have any respect or care for their teachers.

This point is touched on perfectly and thoroughly by Rebecca and Rick in their gripping new book, **_Let Them Speak!_**, especially in their discussion about "Voice Mufflers" in Chapter 1. Respect is all that students have ever wanted from their teachers, and if we receive it, we will give respect back and, in turn, improve our learning by giving ourselves new reasons to crave an education built on engaged learning. We will always support those teachers and educators who genuinely want us to succeed and be our best, but it is so easy for us to be turned off by those who don't want to hear what we have to say about the very learning and teaching going on in our schools.

As my dear student-justice-STEAM-girl-warriors mention repeatedly in this foreword, asking us what we want—and working with what we want and need—will improve everything about our educational system that is meant to service *us*.

A supportive and caring educator is all that a student could ever hope for, which is exactly what Rebecca and Rick are trying to pass on to educators everywhere when making you think about every opportunity to inject student voice into your craft. Their goal is to help teachers with their overall connection with their students, who will ultimately benefit from being heard. I know, for myself, that if my teachers made more of an effort to connect with me and to mold their teaching by taking into consideration what I wanted or needed, I would be more driven to learn and go to school. So, please . . . as a student, I ask you to, at the very least, consider implementing the contents of this book into your professional learning or even alter how you look at your students and work with them. I promise: Your students will thank you for it as they throw their caps into the air and smile in their graduation gowns when they leave you to move on with the rest of their lives. And the reality is, as we move on with life, we will always carry your guidance, knowledge, and care along with us as we try to impact others. Your profession is the greatest profession on earth because you have the potential to impact the world!

"The day I have a voice in my education is the day that I will truly learn."

–Sal

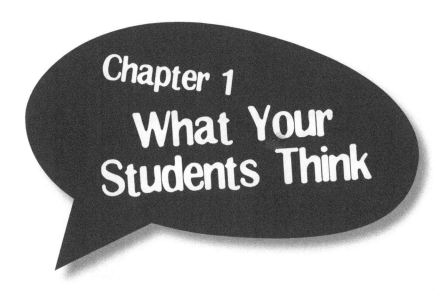

Chapter 1
What Your Students Think

Talk with your children and you will hear
their voices. Walk with them through life
and you will feel their hearts.

—Geoff Reese

What if we told you that students are holding the magic fairy dust that, if added to our educational decision making, could make all the difference in the world? The often repeated cliché is that "truth comes out of the mouths of babes." We believe this cliché has merit and that by talking with students about our schools and then working together through obstacles, we can make schools better.

Think about it: Have you ever heard a student say something that surprised you because it conveyed insightful wisdom and understanding? What if we actively listened to students as if they really were the experts at so many things—things we may never have done or even imagined doing? What do students see that we have missed?

To find out, we can let students speak. It really is that simple. That's what this book is about: listening to students to find the missing links in what we do as educators, using student voices to unveil the mysteries that we might have missed, pointing out the obvious issues, and improving school experiences for all of our students. Students can empower us to make an even bigger difference than we already are making—if we simply ask for their input and let them speak!

ENTERING THE STUDENTS' TURF

Visualize yourself years ago, as a younger student on the elementary school playground or even in high school gym class. Close your eyes for a moment and listen to the echo of sounds as they flood back to the gates of your memory. You hear the screams of joy and laughter while playing a simple game of tag, sneakers squeaking on the gym floor, rhythmic tapping of jump ropes crisscrossing midair, and flags rippling through the air during marching band practice. Student stuff. The *good* stuff. No written objectives, no assigned seating, no lesson plans. You are simply happy being you, a student in school. Positive memories.

What do you recall about your conversations with your friends during your school years? What did you talk about? Were your conversations honest or fake? Chances are you talked about things that were relevant to your life, and other times you laughed about things that were superficial. You probably even had conversations that were connected and authentic. If you were invested, you may have dreamed up ways to improve school if you were "in charge." You may have even talked about your teacher and the things you didn't like about class. Looking back, how did conversations with your friends in school leave you feeling?

Now picture a teacher or principal entering your turf in that same time and space. Maybe you hear the tapping of high heels, walkie-talkie static, a clipboard rapping to the cadence of heavy footsteps, or a whistle being blown at full force. Do you see friendly, welcoming smiles or cold, disapproving stares? Depending on the school experiences that you had, this exercise might remind you of a time when you felt accepted and supported and encouraged to excel in academics, sports, or the arts. For others, it might evoke fear, guilt, disrespect, or the urge to look over your shoulder. Either way, for better or for worse, you were impacted by the way your teachers and principals planned school for you and made decisions about what *they* thought *you* needed. These are the "plotlines" that shaped your experiences and created perceptions of your experiences. We will talk more about "plotlines" later and how they shape identities.

You might have also encountered the need to stop dead in your tracks because bolts of fear surged through your body as you tried to pinpoint what was wrong with school or what was wrong with *you*. An adult might have been on your turf for something as simple as a classmate being picked up early by their mom or dad. Either way, the body language of the adult implied that something was off. Have you encountered a feeling of curiosity or even a "gotcha" feeling that pervaded you while at a pep rally, hanging out in the library, or on your own time at school under the supervision of adults who run the system of learning and leading?

This book is about helping educators better understand the millions of tiny and large impacts that we have on our students, both purposefully and inadvertently, during the craft of being an educator. We will explore the value of examining our mindsets and our interactions with students and the power of truly listening to kids and hearing their perspectives. This book will also outline ways to

Students can do one of three things when approached on their turf: run away, clam up, or open up.

take action to support what students need, not what *we* might perceive *they* need.

THE IMPORTANCE OF TURF

Teachers and principals working in any space within a school should strive to create learning communities where students are accepted, treated fairly, and feel safe enough to take risks. You may have already read *Lead Like a Pirate* by Shelley Burgess and Beth Houf and are now a more approachable and magnetic leader because of the leadership energy that they write about in their book. Your staff and students, even members of the community, can either be genuinely excited or incredibly turned off to see you each day. This idea is essential. Positive culture and climate is the first key ingredient when asking students what they think. Being an approachable leader is the entry point to taking action about what kids tell us they need.

From time to time, educators must approach students in their own space and that means loosening the necktie long enough to join a pick-up game of basketball or joining in on the latest dance craze. Infiltrating student turf, whether it be in the gymnasium before school, in the cafeteria at lunchtime, or in the art room after school, must be unequivocally 100 percent about your students, not you. When we take the time to visit student spaces, we're inviting them to talk with us and share their voices in spaces that aren't stuffy.

Do the students at your school willingly share their thoughts and opinions about school? Are they willing to have an off-the-clock type of conversation with you? What if students knew you were on their turf to ask them a ton of questions about their school as their advocate to empower their point of view—that what they say can be used to help kids enjoy their experiences at school even more than you think they do now? What if *they* knew that *you* wanted to improve the social dynamics and access to learning at their school? How would *they* react? What would *they* say? And what would *they* think?

We believe your students will react with relief, joy, and hope when they see you walk onto their turf with an open mind and the resolve to listen more than you may want to speak.

It's important to remember that these off-the-clock spaces belong to our students. These are the spaces where students have full, personal freedom at school or around the school grounds. When students know it's an honor to have their feedback, entire school communities can move in new directions. Spending time with students on their turf provides the opportunity to have authentic conversations, to ask hard questions, and to share open and honest answers. If you want *real* answers to your school's challenges and dilemmas, students almost always will tell it like it is.

We believe that the most important type of data that we should be collecting and using to improve our schools is *student voice*. And this type of data can be cross-referenced with any other kind of data. Humans should come before numbers. Creating an environment of positive customer service that meets the individual needs of students should dominate the conversations long before achievement data is ever analyzed.

We believe students *do* tell the truth, almost always, and when they are empowered to speak up, what they say can provide useful insights for reforming or transforming your classroom and school. Sometimes it's the adults who clog up the system or make learning harder or more complicated than it needs to be. This is why student voice is so vital to solving school-wide and even global challenges. In many cases, it seems like the obvious answer or missing ingredient, yet we often miss it completely. Incorporating student voice is not easy. It can be uncomfortable and educators have often been too scared to deal with it because accessing student voice has to do with power dynamics. If adults feel that *they* need to be in control, that *they* are to have the power, then we are miserably failing our students.

VOICE MUFFLERS AND VOICE ACTIVATORS

There are varying opinions when it comes to empowering students as change agents within an educational setting. We contend that some adults *muffle* student voice while others *activate* positive change through encouragement. It's not a matter of teachers being nice, kind, or relevant—it has more to do with how they accept students as stakeholders in teaching. Some educators silence student influence and might even believe adults exclusively hold the expertise in schools. Some view students as full participants in their own education who have the right to voice opinions. Both kinds of adults exist in schools, and unless you are tuned in, it might not be evident. Remember, when power is shared, our worlds can become unlocked.

The Voice Mufflers

Voice mufflers are often those teachers and school leaders who don't believe that student voice has the power to improve anything. Or they say student voice is important, but they cross their fingers behind their backs without us seeing it, knowing they really aren't going to do anything about activating student voice. Voice mufflers will go on with their daily business of running their classrooms and schools the way *they* want—the *adult* way. Maybe some educators even asked students to speak up about something but then didn't like what they heard, so they let it fall by the wayside. Some educators believe that kids are loose cannons and simply don't even know what's best for themselves. Others have grown complacent and want to avoid change at all costs, so they're not inclined to listen to student input. This we-know-better-because-we-are-adults mentality can really stifle our schools. This attitude is crippling because it builds a wall that stifles not only student personality and belonging, but also the school's overall ability to grow. Quite honestly, we think this attitude about our students and schools just stinks!

The Voice Activators

Voice activators are a little easier to identify because their energy and excitement are contagious. They make students feel valued and work hard to help everyone be successful in the classroom. Voice activators believe in encouraging student voice and providing the insight necessary to teach and lead with super-high impact. Voice activators believe students deserve good customer service as educational clients and believe in altering adult behavior based on student feedback. Empowering students to improve the system is at the heart of a voice activator.

Which activator do you identify with the most? Why? Which one do you want to identify with moving forward? Which one is most comfortable and natural to you? Which one are you used to? If you don't already consider yourself a voice activator, we challenge you to hear us out—as well as all of your students—before dismissing this approach. We challenge you to read *real* stories from *real* students all across the United States to understand why we are saying, **Let Them Speak!**

STUDENTS ARE OUR CLIENTS

We wondered what our students thought about their schools and figured asking them some specific questions about virtually anything related to their academic success so customer satisfaction could improve. Over the span of three years, we worked at several different schools and visited many more across the nation to foster

There are educators who view students as just that—students. Then there are educators who view students as clients, customers of an education that their parents (the taxpayers) are buying from us. We owe students incredible experiences, or we should be giving them their money back!

an environment in which students trusted and valued our process enough to provide their feedback about school. We wanted to know what irritated them the most about classroom instruction, the biggest challenges they faced, and what inspired them to come to school each day. We gathered story after story from students who were willing to share criticism and praise. Their feedback was inspirational and we consider these young people life-changing voice activators. We believe the experience of exploring kids as clients who deserve exceptional customer service is the missing link that can transform any classroom, school, or district.

TRANSFORMATIONAL NARRATIVES

Educators regularly, or at least periodically, attend megaconferences, and we usually return back to school all fired up. Our buckets get filled with strategies, innovations, and new learnings from colleagues, and it's just the shot in the arm needed to rekindle our pirate passion to capture the status quo and make it walk the plank. Beyond attending conferences, we also read the latest books, join Voxer groups or book studies, and Tweet chat with professionals across the nation. We are all in as educators, pushing boundaries while knowing that our students are counting on us! But, in the aftermath of attending conferences, reading the latest research, and collaborating with our professional learning network, how often do we really put students first right away and then continue doing it until we retire?

We might say that we put kids first, but we may or may not take any action to ensure that this is happening on a daily basis. We might complain that there isn't enough time to do this or that. What if we took what our student clients shared with us and actually put it to use? What if the casual talks about the advice our students give us were captured in writing so that we could archive our students' thoughts and feelings and use their input to further reflect upon our practices at schools everywhere, not just in our own community?

What if we intentionally checked in with our students, gathered their feedback, and used what they say to improve long-standing practices that have grown outdated and ineffective? After all, isn't perceptual, qualitative data on student perspective just as important as quantitative data we gather from testing in the classroom? We sometimes cling to test scores, hoping our students will beat last year's results, but did we ask them anything about the tests they take or the environment in which they learn best?

In reality, we adjust our lessons based on exit tickets and checks for understanding to ensure a perfect lesson. Our lessons are differentiated to meet the instructional needs of all kids in order to make sure they hit all the benchmarks. We have personalized academic data and we reteach and provide additional small-group instruction on the spot, so shouldn't that enough? There are even numerous schools out there using student perception surveys or asking students for written, anonymous feedback. Additionally, many teachers ask their students about their lessons and gather immediate feedback about what they are doing in the classroom. In some areas, school districts have students sit on their school board, school-planning teams, or interview committees. Those approaches certainly foster student voice, but the method we used in the *Let Them Speak!* Project involved listening to students, casually and organically, having them write down their advice or insights, and then using their thoughts as a tool to solve *real* problems in schools. Teachers were able to reflect on the student feedback we gathered to better serve their students. This method is only effective for the voice activators. Voice mufflers will never be successful with this practice, because it requires educators and school leaders to accept student voice and advice in written form, follow up with reflection, and make specific changes to improve the customer service that they should provide in their schools.

THE LET THEM SPEAK! PROJECT

The **Let Them Speak!** Project was inadvertly born in western upstate New York, originally on school playgrounds, as Rick hung out with students and started writing down everything that they had to say. Then he got the kids to write down their thoughts and insights. It didn't start off quite as intentional. At first, it was an organic byproduct of being curious enough to listen to kids. Several years back as a superintendent, Rick had made it a point to visit students in the cafeteria and at recess because it seemed less disruptive than in the classroom during normal instructional time. He wasn't necessarily seeking ways to improve the district; he just discovered that students were honest, real, and relevant in various nonacademic environmental turfs. It was different from the normal teacher-student conversations taking place in the classroom. They wanted to talk, and we mean *they really* wanted to be heard. Time after time, Rick would listen and discover ways to support new or old initiatives and school-wide programs just because he took the time to listen to students. It was a happy accident.

Once Rick discovered he was onto something that could change the direction of the schools and district he worked in, he made it a regular practice to stop by student-turf ecosystems any time he was on a campus doing regular school business. Students were always willing to "tell all" to Rick, and he listened intently and knew he must share these stories with others, so he started having kids write down their recommendations so he could take them along with him in his suitcoat pockets. He continued this practice throughout his principalship and superintendency, and held on to those student vignettes that he knew would one day change schools forever.

Fast-forward to the end of 2016. We had just cowritten *Escaping the School Leader's Dunk Tank*—a book primarily for school leaders. During the writing process, we had so many conversations about school improvement topics ranging from technology to school culture to curriculum to building relationships. We were boundary pushers and dreamers dialoging about school improvement. During a phone conversation while we were both driving into work one day, Rick shared his practice of meeting kids on their turfs. That very same day, Rebecca decided to put student voice into practice within her own district!

She decided to start first with a challenging adolescent grade level, and headed out to a seventh-grade recess/free-time period. From her first day on the job of activating student voice, intentionally on her students' turf ecosystems, Rebecca learned the value of listening for student voice about all sorts of topics. She asked questions that other adults never took the time to ask. From that day forward, Rebecca also collected vignettes, sometimes holding on to them until a door opened wide enough with the adults to bring it up, and other times sharing those amazing stories at faculty meetings. Student voice became such a focus because it was leading to actual improvements within the sometimes stiff walls of the educational system.

We continued dialoging with each other about our stories of triumphs (and sometimes trials or burdens that students faced) and even met with other educators along the way who were also just as passionate and willing to participate in this innovative practice. It was a game changer for sure. This was just the beginning of the *Let Them Speak!* Project.

We loved the social and emotional dynamic of student spaces, and we were able to get to know students on a different level. From the cafeteria, playground, and library to the nurses' offices, classroom stations, hallways, and so many other places, we stopped and listened to students while we were visitors in *their* ecosystems. It's a relationship builder, an investment, and a good practice to become allies with students. We discovered issues that were impacting groups of students in different areas of so many different schools, and we heard about misconceptions or fears that students had about taking tests or learning new math concepts. We learned a lot just from listening. What we noticed most about what students were willing to share with us was that their perspectives were *profound*.

As former writing teachers, we were both motivated to go one step further with what we heard from students. From time to time, when their input altered our thinking, we would ask students to write down their thoughts. What we were asking them to do was transform their spoken words into tangible, written documents of empowerment. We wanted something we could forward in an email or photocopy and pass out to share with other adults. We found these written pieces expressed innovation, changes, and considerations and brought a new level of clarity to the impact of our educational leadership.

By extending the conversation to a written artifact, the students' feedback became a framework for discussion for everyone affected by a particular issue. And so, the project was born through this type of historicized archive—a digital closet where narratives could be labeled with pseudonyms if kids were worried about speaking up, where writing triggered sweeping changes and reforms because it made voices stand out on paper for any adult in any nook and cranny of our globe to think about how to improve their classrooms and schools.

We had the chance to talk with students in every grade level, Pre-K through twelfth grade. For entertainment value, the younger the student, the more they had to say about everything! And yes, their stories were transcribed—some even accompanied by cute drawings or sketches.

So, we got to thinking: Why their turf? We defined *their* turf as any unstructured area where they had choice and freedom rather than an assignment or regularly scheduled objective or responsibility. Places like recess, lunch, hallways, the library, and even the gym while waiting for an assembly to start—these were places of common time, communal time, more relaxed time. Turf ecosystems are places where students are not expected to perform, but rather just be *themselves*. What makes these spaces so rich with honesty and insight? Well, these are places that are informal, casual, relaxed, playful, and spirited. It takes the teacher or leader out of the classroom filled with desks, books, and shelves or the office filled with paperwork, voicemail, and to-do lists and places students at the forefront of their own domains. The time and space of students' actual *turf* requires acceptance and trust. Or, at least initial compliance.

What was really nice about hanging out on student-turf ecosystems is that fresh perspectives positively impacted our attitudes. No formalities. No holding back. No precautions. No rules. Just the power of communication, understanding, and the respect that each has for one another, leader to learner and learner to leader. Student turf is where peers talk to peers—well, at least most of the time. It's where students hang out when school isn't in session, and it's where they let out some energy during the school day when they are blessed with teachers who believe in free time and recess. Student turf represents memorable life events, sometimes signifying a fight with a friend or where a first kiss took place.

Let Them Speak!

Our students felt compelled enough to talk with us about their own beliefs, feelings, and emotions regarding the classrooms and schools that they inhabit each day. Student turf is different than the formal spaces in the school building because when students talk, they share different things that they might not share with educators had they not been asked on their own terms. On their turfs, their guards are down, and their brutal honesty isn't judged by a peer or anyone else, for that matter. Students willingly shared their fears with us as well. The dynamic is just different in their spaces of the school.

What we also noticed is that students often talked about people (both positively and negatively, of course). They got stuff off their chests. They played or chilled out, yes, but the student ecosystem is also a place where students *confide* in one another as equals. That's where *they* bond. That's where they go to try to stay out of trouble. It's a safe place, whether it is a park, athletic event, or playground. It's a fun place. It's a place where students can be themselves. Even when students are just sitting around, messing around, enjoying the sun and friendships with no cares in the world, that's where they want to be and even be heard. In their own time and space, students can be who they really want to be. That's where we wanted to gather our stories, the most authentic settings where we could get the most honest answers without the formal artifacts of school staring at them in the face and reminding them that they are governed by adults who are listening, watching, or even telling on them or getting them in trouble. So that's where we headed to gather our stories of authenticity: *their turfs*. We entered this ecosystem of students' turfs, whether it was the school community gardens, gazebos, student lounges, football fields, basketball courts, playgrounds, or tennis courts and we kept going and going and going with our passion to collect student voices.

We all have "plotlines" in our lives, and these plotlines shape who we are, what we think, and what we have been through. Plotlines create and renovate our identities, which are always in motion and change at the drop of a hat. Plotlines can change us for better or for worse, but all it takes is a magnificent act or incident to smother a negative experience, and we want to smother our students with amazing, memory-changing, life-altering plotlines. All we are doing is killing our students' identities if we ignore what they say as they create new plotlines.

Let Them Speak!

Student and Educator Plotlines

We accumulated more than seventy-five hours of turf-ecosystem visits between the two of us, and we learned so much from every ecosystem that we visited. As we shared our experiences, we started to notice commonalities. We noticed that over time and across various states, no matter the age, socioeconomic level, race, gender, or grade level of the student, that three perceptual types of plotlines existed among students and educators in our schools:

1. What children think about their school and their educational experiences
2. What adults think about their school and instructional or leadership experiences
3. What adults think their students think about their school and educational experiences

The third plotline is where things can get messy. There is no blame intended here, but we are so busy, as adults, that it's easier to assume what students think (based on our own schema) rather than take the time to find out what our students actually think (about everything). Our time is consumed with preparing lessons, attending meetings, balancing our careers and lives, and so many other factors that get away from us each day. It's vital to remember that being a voice activator and asking students about their opinions takes both time and committed effort.

We were committed, no matter what got in the way, to bridge the gap that we saw in our own schools regarding the third plotline that we listed above. We resolved to truly make students the center of our lives and careers. We didn't use slogans such as "kids first," "student-centered environment," or "in the best interests of students" without taking some sort of action. We all believe that, but some of us don't really walk the walk, as we've already discussed. Sometimes we operate in a vacuum even if we don't mean to. For this book, we walked the walk, and when we did, we were able to move student turf advice into the classroom. We worked with students on how to find their voices, write down their thoughts, and make us the believers in a new and improved student faith that has gone unnoticed by some educators for far too long.

It has to start with us. Grassroots movements can work. It doesn't have to be a top-down effort to make a positive impact. We must become such a loud and positive grassroots movement of listening to student voice that the community cannot help but notice our schools' improvements. This is our *why*. Our students are counting on us. It's why we write, why we spend our time off planting seeds about student voice, and why we present this topic at conferences that believe in voice activators even if voice mufflers are sitting in the audience. We believe too deeply in this message to not do our best to alter the perceptions of educators across the nation.

In our book *Escaping the School Leader's Dunk Tank*, we gathered hundreds of stories from school leaders across the nation regarding how they face adversity in their careers and how they prevail both as leaders and human beings. Their stories resonated with us. Stories evoke emotion. Now, if we were moved by these adult stories, wait until you see the stories from students across the nation in the following chapters. It is powerful to read, and we guarantee that some sort of emotion will be evoked from you when you read this collection of student narratives in the following chapters. If we take the time to value adult voice and adult stories, we must take the time to mine for student voice and student stories. Not only is it fair, but it is what is right!

Be genuine. Be remarkable. Be worth connecting with.

–Seth Godin

Breaking Down Barriers

During our fieldwork, we reported to our real "offices"—the student-turf ecosystems—a few times each week. We didn't invade; in fact, they didn't know what we were doing. We were just there hanging out, or we were assigned a duty in that area, perhaps, and came and went as we pleased. Or we visited a colleague's school to gather student voice data and, if we saw students having fun, we usually didn't interrupt. We shied away from intrusion. If we saw an opportunity to talk with a student, we sat alongside them, gathering information on how we were doing with our customer service. Sometimes our students wanted to talk with us nonstop about anything and everything. On occasion, students were too cool or felt awkward and didn't want to talk, so we just gave a word of encouragement and respected their space. Other times, we prompted students by joking around and first establishing trust. Whether students were eager or reluctant to talk, if we didn't have a specific topic in mind, we stuck to these six questions to ensure we were staying focused on the goal of increasing customer service and instigating *real* reform within our schools:

1. What don't we, as educators, understand about you, the students, at this school?
2. What is something that you wish we could do better?
3. What have we failed to recognize about you or your experience as a student at our school?
4. Is there anything that upsets you about our school that we should fix, rethink, eliminate, or no longer ignore?
5. What do you value the most about your learning experiences at our school?
   ⁶w do you feel the night before coming to school on a new
   a weekend, or after a holiday or summer vacation?

We historicize anything verbal into narrative text so it breathes realism from the very first whisper and is not forgotten.

Let Them Speak!

The **Let Them Speak!** Project then intentionally grew and continued on the foundation of these six questions even before talking with any new students because we knew what we wanted to continue doing after it proved amazing results for *our* schools.

From Oral to Written Stories

Years ago, we both remember reading *Fires in the Bathroom* by Kathleen Cushman. These were urban stories, stories from the streets, stories that pulled at your heartstrings, important stories, stories untold that would help educators better understand their students. *The Freedom Writers Diary* was Erin Gruwell's story (then to be made a movie starring Hilary Swank) about writing with passion, writing with heart, and telling a story that would create legendary history in the worlds of students' lives. Street-wise and street-smart writing. What these types of urbanized, epic stories did was pump blood through students' veins and jerk the tears right from teachers' eyes. These stories were motivational. Unconventionally motivational. And they worked. They worked to improve systems. Those stories gathered teachers to take a stand and moved education forward with storytelling at its core and writing as a product of archiving and triggering incredible reflection and practical methods. There is power in writing because every student has a story to be told.

What if we shared with you that when we talked to students on playgrounds or other turf ecosystems across the United States and gathered insights from amazing students who lit up our lives, we wanted to take them and their thoughts into classrooms where desks were stabilized for writing so they could write their own narratives? What students did after talking to us was enter into a craft of writing so that they could write history that would change their teachers, principals, and schools forever. We wanted to know how students could enter into our worlds, write from their student plotlines, and archive the experiences where they know best.

Students spend more time in school than at home (most times). We have a duty to invite their perspectives and wisdom to transform the writing process into a written discovery of their innermost worlds unknown to educators. Their methods of teaching us their own personally contextualized writing from the soul . . . extracted from their turfs . . . come from the hearts of those who bite their tongues and simply comply with what we are doing in their classrooms so they can receive a grade and move on.

From Turf to Classroom

This book is not about helping you teach narrative writing. It is focused on capturing the student voice that can come through when students share with us what they think and feel about the schools they attend. We would like to contribute to the world of wonder for our students as we permit ultimate expression through oral storytelling and the narrativization of students' oral stories. We want them to tell us something about their lives, their classrooms, or their schools we didn't know before. Adults have different perceptions about education and sometimes those don't match our students' innovative and complex viewpoints.

When we hit the pavement of visiting students' turfs, our process was simple:

1. We engaged in small talk, which led to more open talk about more serious subjects. Plus, we love to joke around, so getting students to laugh a little bit was a memorable experience for us.
2. We often had food in hand to share with our students. You won't believe how far a bag of Skittles goes with creating

Any problem, any issue, any quandary, or any adversity can always be solved with a little student-voice elbow grease.

a bond between a teacher and a student beyond the classroom walls. We know, you might be antisugar and antibribery, but we love Skittles, and it seemed to work for us.

3. If students had something to tell us, we would let them lead the discussion, and often times their self-prompted stories raised our eyebrows about things that seemed out of whack in our schools—things we could fix with a little student-voice elbow grease.

4. If students didn't know in what direction they wanted to go, we would use one of the prompts outlined earlier.

5. If students were still stuck on what to think about or reflect on with one of those prompts, we delved deeper into linking the prompts with a specific area—hence the reason why the chapters in this book are what they are. Topics such as antibullying, policies, politics, instruction, grading, homework, motivation, discipline, safety, and assessment were thrown around as topics to spark ideas or push students to think about all that goes on inside and outside of school.

6. When students opened up with a great story, we took quick notes while they chatted with us. The notes were then handed off to the students at the end of our visit, and they took them to the classroom to recreate and transcribe so we could historicize their voices.

7. No fuss. No mess. No formalized writing instruction needed. Just oral-to-written narrative so the adults in our students' lives could wrestle with a new reality.

One teacher, Elana Mills from Philadelphia, thought that what we were doing—gathering students' voices and stories from student turf and ecosystems—was a type of *treason* against the schools that work so hard to establish safe and caring learning environments.

Elana was a "no-nonsense" teacher who laid the law down in her classroom. It was her way or the highway. She was in charge. Never would she have thought of turning power over to her students.

Treason? Hmm . . . maybe we'll use that word and concept to develop our understanding about utilizing student voice!

If this be treason, make the most of it!

–Patrick Henry

BUILDING A CULTURE OF HEALTHY TREASON

Elana was right. There is a form of treason going on in **Let Them Speak!**, but it is a healthy treason that can be reflective for educators everywhere. Consider Erica Wilkins, a sixth-grade teacher we both know and admire. She's an excellent teacher, and here's why: One day we took Erica out to her school playground with us. We sat with a few students on the swings, and while shuffling our feet through the mulch underneath our sneakers, we asked some of the students the following question: "What can we do to make your life in school *happier*?"

"Happier? Give me a break. Sometimes, kids aren't going to like everything they have to do in school," said one of Erica's colleagues, as she overheard Erica chatting with us about the need to know more about what our students think about everything that we do.

We believe learning can and should always be enjoyable, and so do most students. So why is there, sometimes, a disconnect between adults' expectations of school and students' expectations of school?

Jonah, a fifth grader in a different class; Sarah, a sixth grader in one of Erica's classes; and Rodney, a fourth grader in a different class, all gathered around and told us the truth about our question regarding *happiness* in school. Check out the conversation that we had with these amazing kids:

Jonah: I know what you could do for us . . . get rid of homework.

Rodney: Yeah, you teachers think we just want to get out of doing homework, but there is more to it than that.

Sarah: You got that right. After school, I come home after picking up my little brother, Dustin, from school. I go home to cook dinner for him while my mom is at work, I help him with his homework, and then by the time I have to get to mine, I'm tired and end up falling asleep. No one says it's easy being a kid. Everyone thinks we just want to get out of doing homework or because when we don't do it or turn it in late, it's because we don't care. But, no one cares to ask me what my night is like.

Rebecca: You're like a mom to Dustin while your mom is at work, huh?

Rick: And your teachers have no clue about that?

Erica: Oh my God, Sarah, I'm so sorry. I wish I knew all that about you, hon. You know I really care about ya, kid. You can tell me anything . . . you know that, right?

Sarah: Nothing to be sorry about, Miss W.; that's just my life. My mom gives us a good life; it's just that she works the second shift and isn't home when we come home. Homework complicates the responsibilities we have at home and in our home life. Speaking up about homework doesn't really do a whole lot for us. It hinders more than helps us. My teachers assign me detention when I don't do my homework, but I can't stay because I have to pick my brother up from school. Then, when I miss detention, it leads to in-school suspension. I have a "record" because when I miss detention, it shows up on my transcript and my teachers think I'm a bad kid when they see me during in-school suspension or have me in their class the following year.

Erica asked Sarah if she would be willing to write down her thoughts about homework and how it personally impacted her and her family. Sarah agreed, but Erica knew she couldn't let the conversation end there. This caused Erica to wonder if other students were also dealing with the same issues. The following day, at the end of her school's faculty meeting, and without mentioning Sarah's name, Erica read Sarah's story out loud to everyone present. She was determined to gain allies and talk through alternatives for this school-wide practice that was negatively impacting kids. What she discovered was that many other students were also struggling with homework because of their home life.

The only guideline Erica had given Sarah for the narrative was to keep it appropriate for school. The first-person account was emotional and raw, outlining exactly why homework had not only made Sarah's daily life more difficult, but had also become counterproductive to her overall education. While many of the staff members were nodding their heads in agreement, a few rolled their eyes. The fourth-grade team of teachers chimed in and shared that they were reading *Ditch that Homework* by Matt Miller and Alice Keeler. The team was excited to share incredible alternatives to homework. You could read the body language of the resistant teachers who loved giving homework. The principal even stepped in at one point to mediate the healthy dialogue that was taking place. After all, it was quite a mind shift for the resistant teachers to make based on one simple student narrative. The principal did an eloquent job of bringing the conversation back to the student narrative and meeting the needs of students.

This plotline demonstrates how every student has a voice. But like Erica, we can't let it stop there. Educators must encourage their students to use their voices by writing down their narratives for the purpose of affecting change at their schools. We are grateful to Jonah,

Rodney, and Sarah for sharing their voices, but if we hadn't been looking for them, would we have landed on such a hot mess that needed sorting out? Sooner or later, the real-life burdens of homework and the school's overall philosophy about homework might have surfaced. Then again, it might not have ever come up without student voice activating the issue.

Long story short, homework is no longer a priority at Cactus Rose Elementary School. The school leaders came to an understanding that it wasn't essential to passing to the next grade and developed other ways to hold students accountable for their learning. By simply asking students how to make their school experience happier, the *Let Them Speak!* Project helped one school make a change—reshaping its homework policy—that will benefit thousands and thousands of students for years to come.

In the end, Sarah's words—first spoken and then transformed into a written narrative—became a discussion point for her entire school community. Teachers wanted to read her narrative and students wanted to share their stories. Perhaps for the first time in her life, Sarah believed that her story, her voice, and her opinions mattered. And all it took was an adult showing up in her life and asking a simple question that triggered amazing outcomes!

Collecting your students' stories and helping them share their narratives is not a classroom project or a routine assignment. It is an authentic, organic conversation that is focused on student customer service. When any issue surfaces, and a student articulates a meaningful perspective, we talk about it and have them write down their thoughts. It doesn't mean that every student in the conversation must be assigned a writing project. Erica asked Sarah to share her story in writing because it was so compelling. There will be times when you might want several students to write a narrative, but that isn't always necessary. Capturing even one student's perspective in writing so that it can be shared with other adults in a problem-solving setting is where the magic comes into play.

In staying true to our belief in the power of student perspective and influence, we couldn't have moved forward with this book without securing student approval. So we shared our early manuscript of this book with Isaiah Sterling, a student in Missouri who has a powerful social media voice and leads educators nationwide as the founder of #weleadby. We wanted real, honest student truth and, boy, did he reframe our initial project! He provided us with an altogether new perspective and direction. Our original title for this book was *Stories from the Playground* with a cover design that depicted kids having fun on a playground. To Isaiah, a high school student, the image did not resonate with older kids. He was right. It was an early-childhood concept and not inclusive of all students at every level. We valued his student voice, digested all the recommended changes, and altered the direction of this book so that everyone had a stake in the outcome. We headed back to the drawing board, and eventually **Let Them Speak!** emerged, thanks to Isaiah pushing us to think more about our work and our audience. His powerful and relevant insights about the student turfs beyond playgrounds helped us to extract student voice in so many other ecosystems as we described earlier. He even helped us in our decision regarding the cover of this book. Initially, we had envisioned an image of students' mouths being unzipped. But when we showed the cover concepts to Isaiah, his discomfort with those images compelled us to rethink our ideas. Taking his point of view into account, we agreed with him about the creepiness of unzippered mouths. It looked too nightmarish, indeed!

Because you are reading this book—and you are most likely an exceptional educator or leadership-minded educator—and have stuck with us to the end of the first chapter, you are surely one of the good ones. You are a treasure hunter who believes every student

"Giving in" and "turning over your power" are mindsets of faulty systems, not innovative, caring educators. If you want to be somebody else, then change your mind. Push back on the very systems that strangle your students' voices, and you will find a pot of gold, shiny and new.

is capable of success. You probably Tweet, Vox, and SnapChat with the most innovative educators, plan meticulously, and use your PLN to connect with other innovators. You genuinely put students first and encourage them to speak up about the issues that affect their education.

But consider this: Are you approaching your students on their own turf—the basketball court, the mall, the cafeteria, the empty lot across from their school—where they feel comfortable enough to answer your questions about teachers, discipline, dress codes, tests, and anything else that comes up? Are you willing to let students take the baton and lead the way to progress and reflection?

JUST GIVE STUDENTS EVERYTHING THEY WANT?

This book isn't about "giving kids everything they want." As adults, *we* don't even get everything that *we* want, and sometimes we don't even know why we want something, anyway. Often, we forget to think about the domino effect of our actions or take time to deeply analyze what we need, why we need it, or what is driving a need in the first place. We can easily forget that the desired outcome of using student voice can be replicated everywhere. Reflection takes time.

At the BET-C in Phoenix in October 2017, we presented *Let Them Speak!* for the first time. During our session, one of the educators in our audience gave us the following scenario and posed a very interesting question for us to answer while also letting us know how the situation was resolved at his own school. Here is what Jarod Farrow, a high school counselor in Arizona, shared with us about student voice and the quandary about simply giving students (or giving in to students) everything that they request:

So, last week I had this student named Mindy come to me and request getting out of a particular teacher's class. She said that the teacher was allegedly a terrible teacher . . . that Mindy didn't like him . . . that she just wanted out. I could have moved Mindy based on her request, but I thought about her concerns a little more deeply: too much homework, looks at her funny, doesn't give her a chance to answer questions in class. What was even more interesting is that some of Mindy's friends heard that she was asking to be moved and they came down to my office in order to request a teacher change as well. I thought to myself: Is this a conspiracy? Is the teacher really acting this way? Why do these students not like their teacher? My gut reaction would have been to not give them their way, but there was something more here. I had to discern the difference between what was real, factual, perceived, and possibly broken. It didn't seem like a conspiracy. But, it could have been. I shared this with my principal and here is how he handled it: He brought all five students, Mindy being one of them, into his office, closed the door, asked about their concerns, and had an explicit conversation with them about making their school experience a better experience versus "taking a tire off of the car completely and letting the school ride on three wheels." What was interesting here is what happened next. While the students did not want their teacher to know that they didn't like him, the principal had a meeting with their teacher and then set up an additional meeting with the students to review what steps would be taken to address their concerns without giving them the feeling that they could ask for and just simply receive anything that they wanted in school or life. My principal laid out a very explicit plan that would have the teacher reflect on homework policies, letting them have voice in class by answering questions, and not making them feel uncomfortable in any way. The teacher actually didn't know that his students felt that way. He didn't know that Mindy didn't like class, since she was doing well and had one of the highest math grades in the tenth grade. What it did was give students the comfort of using their voice while explaining an explicit process that would be taken to address concerns. This is what I admired most. The students seemed satisfied that their concerns weren't swept under the rug. Someone cared. Someone listened to them. I didn't jump to conclusions by giving Mindy and her friends what they thought they wanted when they marched into my office.

When students feel like we care, know that we care, and hear about a process that we are going to take, explicitly, to solve a problem or troubleshoot a situation, they respect us more. At least, in our experiences and talking with students and educators across the nation, what might seem like *irrational knee-jerk requests* can truly become *rational dialogues* that engage students to think about bridging perceptions between child and adult in order to learn more about their worlds of needs, wants, and quick feelings of how they think they should solve any problem.

We have a duty to explicitly teach students about the process of looking at problems from all angles, and it doesn't necessarily mean that we "give everyone everything that they want" at any time. What it *does* mean in this book and in our understanding of student voice is that a comfort zone is created for students and that their voices are heard, valued, and respected about anything—so long as we teach them that solving a problem or looking at a situation is multidimensional, not acute, swift, or always easy. And our answer to Jarod during our presentation covered just that.

Voice Activator Reflections

In what ways can you encourage healthy treason in your classroom? How can you foster a grassroots movement in your school that seeks to access and activate student voice? Where will you start, and what issues can be presented to students for their feedback?

Chapter 2
Kids Share Zingers and Stingers

Wisdom ceases to be wisdom when it becomes too proud to weep, too grave to laugh, and too selfish to seek other than itself.

–Khalil Gibran

As we had more and more conversations with students on their turf, the *Let Them Speak!* Project started taking a shape of its own—sometimes pushing us to listen to the truths that might make us squirm the most. These informal conversations and their narratives led us to a personal and reflective place. When students of any age share any unadulterated truth, we owe it to them to raise the bar and actively listen. Initially, we might not be inclined to do what is right if we don't like what we hear. Putting students' needs first requires educators to alter their behaviors and even embrace that which is most uncomfortable. Whether looking at standardized test scores, shuffling students around for Response to Intervention (RtI) strategies, or facing problems with school initiatives, students hold

The only true wisdom is knowing that you know nothing.

—Socrates

the key that could unlock the mysteries that adults sometimes miss. That's why we must be brave enough to ask, open enough to listen, and wise enough to act when student voice is activated.

We will always be role models, whether we are teaching "like pirates," innovating with cross-curricular project-based lessons, or simply leading a regimented phonics routine with fidelity. Our students are always watching us. Always. One of the main differences between being an exceptional educator and being an average educator is choosing to listen to our students.

Historically, education has been symbiotic. If you rewind the history of education, itself, all the way back to its Socratic roots, the greatest of philosophers intended to learn as much from their students as their students learned from them. Our modern-day use of Socratic Circles and Philosophical Chairs is evidence that this idea has clearly stood the test of time.

We must return to such philosophical roots and listen with the intent of allowing students to enlighten us. The fact that you made an active decision to read this book is a good indicator that you are most likely a transformational educator who already professes not to know everything. Hold on to this idea of enlightenment as your students throw you what we call "zingers and stingers"—or things that breathe brutal honesty where pain should be distilled and transformed into healing. Be willing to rethink your own leadership as you work at being a voice activator.

DOOR #5

Consider this dialogue between Jason, a fifth grader from New York, and his principal, Doug Patterson, regarding a new dismissal plan. The new plan requires students to exit the school at the end of the day using only designated doors that were chosen by the adults at the school (for security purposes, or so they claimed):

Jason: Mr. Patterson, why can't I leave school out Door #5 anymore? That's where my mom meets me.

Mr. Patterson: Jay, we designed the new procedure to keep students safe.

Jason: But what is unsafe about Door #5?

Mr. Patterson: Well, that's a . . . that's a good question. See, we don't have enough adults to be at those back doors. We need supervision at all of our dismissal doors.

Jason: But what is so unsafe? What could happen? Door #5 is not near the parking lot. It's back by the bike path where lots of kids go to walk home. Door #2 and Door #3 are in the front of the building where the buses go. Aren't those more unsafe than Door #5 because they are where the buses are driving around? Plus, I have to go all the way around the building outside to still head back to the bike path to meet my mom there, anyway, since we walk across the field path to get to our house.

Mr. Patterson: Well, that's just the way we designed the new plan so we can have all the students exiting the building in the same spot to keep an eye on everyone. Understand?

Jason: No, I don't understand. But OK. Bye. See you tomorrow.

After Jason left for the day, Doug had two choices:

1. He could have moved on with the rest of his day and other work that he needed to finish.

-OR-

2. He could have reflected on his conversation with Jason.

Doug intentionally went back to his office to think about his conversation with Jason. He knew he hadn't given Jason a good reason or explanation about the new dismissal plan. It didn't make any sense. It was an adult plan that didn't service students properly. And Jason was right—Door #5 *was* safer than the front doors of the school. After a few days of using the new dismissal plan, after noticing incredible congestion in front of the school, and after seeing a student almost get hit by a bus, Doug designed another plan for dismissal. This time he invited some students and parents to offer their input. Jason became part of the decision-making team at his elementary school. Jason singlehandedly pushed back on a procedure he believed wasn't well thought out, but he wasn't disrespectful about it. He wasn't a rebellious treasonist; he was a *healthy* treasonist. And, his voice changed the way the school dismissal ran and functioned for everyone's safety.

ADULT INTENTIONS AND STUDENT REALITIES

In this next story, Kim Hayes, a teacher in New Jersey, isn't afraid to hear truths, perceptions, or insights from her students. In fact, she was the main catalyst for this chapter. We wrestled with putting this chapter together because it is so unorthodox, but to really portray the power of student voice, we decided that we had to go into spaces where others don't go.

One day, Kim walked out to the track at her school—where her students often walked and talked after lunch—and we tagged along. She asked her middle school students the following questions:

- Do you ever feel like telling a teacher or staff member what you really think about all of the things we do or say in school that drive you nuts?
- Do you ever feel like some decisions or rules don't make sense to you or don't actually work when they are implemented?

- Do you ever feel like you, the students, are not placed at the top of what we do and why we do it here at our school?

Kim opened the communication floodgates on her students' turf. She asked for it. She dared them to practice healthy treason. She would shoulder the criticism, blame, or shame. She didn't care, because she knew that something had to change at her school regarding all of the things that are done without student input. What she cared about was extracting student voice. Kim wanted to help transform her school by delving into some of its biggest problems, and she knew some of the conversations might sting, but the discomfort was worth it. She facilitated a respectful discussion that we applaud. Here is what Kim uncovered about superintendent conference days:

> I actually want to go to school when we have off for a conference day or something. It's hard for me to eat when I'm not at school. I get good meals at school. And my friends are there, too. I don't mind reading and writing. It is very peaceful and calming compared to my mom fighting with her stupid boyfriend all the time at my house. I was hanging out at the store with my compadres and I saw my teachers having lunch in a diner near my school. When they left, I went to school to see if I could hang out with them—even help around the classroom, if they wanted me to. I wasn't really doing anything special, anyway. So I went even though I knew that they were supposed to do some professional development stuff—at least that's what they told me a superintendent's conference day was. But when I got there, my teachers were just hanging out in their classrooms, laughing, and messing around. I asked them if I could hang out with them too, and they said it was cool with them. They put me to work lifting boxes and tidying up their rooms. They even gave me their leftover food from lunch that sat in Styrofoam containers on their

desks. And they weren't doing anything really important, anyway. They said they were going to grade papers, but maybe they did, like, one or two or something.

—Terrence, Grade 6

Terrence spoke up. Certainly he doesn't have all the information about the staff development day. Maybe there were workshops in the morning or maybe the teachers had an agreement with their principal to use time after lunch to grade papers. But instead of being defensive about what Terrence was saying, Kim took these words to heart and shared this narrative with several of her colleagues. After they got past the sting of appearing to "not do anything important," the conversation about Terrence and his true needs changed—in a good way. Kim asked Terrence if he would write down what he told her so that she could share the information with others to improve their school. He agreed.

Kim and her close colleagues read Terrence's narrative and reflected on how they were truly spending the gift of time and learning on staff development days. They made a pact to utilize having fun together, but also to hold each other accountable for meeting the needs of all kids by not wasting time that could better be served by learning and growing in new ways.

Kids see things for what they are, pure and simple. Terrence was looking at the situation through the eyes of a middle school student who had no agenda and no reason to not call things the way that he saw them. For him, the teacher workday meant a day with no food, no security, and nothing to do. Terrence was surprised to see his teachers just hanging out, and he spoke up about his perception. He wasn't calculating a moment to deliver a zinger. His teachers asked, he answered, and they listened. They also took action by using Terrence's narrative to refine and reform their own teacher workday practices.

Kim took Terrence's narrative beyond her own colleagues and shared it with her principal, Tyson Briggs, who used it to make his school's staff development days count more than ever before. This narrative even ignited the idea to have every teacher bring just one story from a child's turf to their next PD day.

The educators in Tyson's and Kim's school could have taken offense to Terrence's narrative, but they didn't. In fact, they used it as a motivational tool to plan one of the best staff development days that they had ever. And this time, students were part of planning the day and leading the day. Terrence didn't have to worry about where to go or what to eat that day because he was the honored guest. He was the reason everything mattered, the reason improvements were made to the school. They replaced grading papers and going out for a long lunch with showcasing student work that would drive initiatives and change, all while dining with their students, *together*, so they could learn *together*.

Examining the Plotlines

Throughout this book, we will invite you to review the perceptions of our students and adults, which we call "plotlines." We all live through plotlines that define our position and frame our constantly changing identity. It is through plotlines that we can change what we believe and how we act. According to Lev Vygotsky, the identity of a teacher or principal can change due to the dualistic relationship of the "other" having a dramatic impact on the "self." Let's take Terrence's narrative and look at the plotline differences to examine how the **Let Them Speak!** Project created major shifts in status quo school practices.

The Student Voice Plotline: "What are you doing that is so important that I have to miss school? Do you know that when I'm

Handle yourself in such a way that when your students think of integrity and equity, they think of you.

not in school, I'm not taken care of? Do you know that you are the best role model in my life?"

What We Need to Consider: During professional development days, are we maximizing time together as colleagues? How can we best honor students with our time on early release or PD days?

Voice Activator Reflections: Don't be a victim to the clock or routine that you think you need to follow. Are there moments when free time governs your day during prep or before or after school? What can be done to reflect on the activities that are meaningless versus leveraging the ones that could be more meaningful to get rid of things that don't make any sense?

PLANNING PERIOD DEMANDS

Cindy Patterson, a fifth-grade teacher in Ohio, learned a lot about herself through her student, Monique. After a turf session—eating lunch together in the courtyard outside the cafeteria—Monique opened up to her teacher about the things that drove her nuts as a student. Monique shared how Ms. Patterson's behavior appeared to be lacking some professionalism. The misbehavior took place during an end-of-the-year, school-wide field day. The fifth-grade students had worked hard all year and met their high-achievement reading goals and were celebrating their success. Nearly the entire grade level was either reading on grade level or above grade-level expectations. It was a well-deserved reward for all. Not even thinking about the field day the day prior, Monique made a distinct observation about how her teacher had acted. Cindy had to use every ounce of restraint to not react with facial expressions or get angry or cry. It was difficult, but she simply listened. Then she asked Monique to write down her story:

We had an end-of-the-year school picnic, so our schedule for the day changed. All I know is I saw my teacher flip out on my principal because she wanted her planning period back and wanted him to cover her being able to leave the barbecue for forty-five minutes. She even used the "G" word—grievance. I might just be a kid, but I know what a grievance is—especially since I have heard her say it before when she was talking to the other teachers about all of the contract stuff going on with the teachers. I gotta be honest. She looked so foolish and it made me feel like she cared more about getting a break than spending time with us. What did she have to plan for in the last week of school, anyway? We all know the last weeks of school are just fun. It made me feel like she was done with us, like she had too high of a dose of us kids or something. We are nice kids. We just wanted to enjoy the day and enjoy it with our teacher. We worked hard to meet this goal. I felt like we didn't even matter. What is forty-five minutes anyway?

—Monique, Grade 5

Monique's teacher most certainly could have had something important to do during her planning period. Maybe there was an important meeting or phone call that needed to be made. Maybe Monique's teacher had to run out to see her sick child or maybe she had an important errand to run. Perhaps she was just having a bad day and that was the straw that broke the camel's back. There are always reasons for every human behavior.

Sometimes the student voice plotlines aren't what we want to hear. They can seem disrespectful, but one thing is for sure: Monique heard everything and noticed that her teacher was mad at her principal about the full-day schedule. For Monique, it was time that her teacher desired to spend away from her and her classmates. Right or wrong, that was her perception. Maybe the teacher's union had a good reason to push for what it contractually should receive. In any event, Monique's teacher reflected on what students should not be exposed to and was reminded that adult conversations should take place behind closed doors.

Examining the Plotlines

Perceptions are valid. Monique felt the way she felt and rightly so. Examining plotlines and stepping into another perspective or role can alter our mindsets enough to make us think twice before an incident takes place.

The Student Voice Plotline: "I can hear the things you say, even if you don't think I can hear them. I feel less important than your planning period. You might have something very important to do, but we want to have lunch with you and enjoy the day with you. I will miss you during the summer because I love having you as my teacher. Why can't you just stay with us and celebrate without demanding some time away from us?"

What We Need to Consider: Our students listen when we speak, and something they might overhear us saying can have a lasting impact on them. Our words can hurt their feelings, whether it's our intention or not. Educators are humans. We make mistakes. We give ourselves to our profession, and we spend endless amounts of time at school working to help children every day. Without meaning any harm, we might poke fun at our students' writing or math inadequacy or something else they could overhear. If anything, when we decide to activate student voice, our students remind us to think, reflect, listen, and examine what we do and say in the presence of them. Their stories are fresh and bold, but they can be helpful when we look at how to create a culture where professional boundaries exist, but students are still celebrated at all times.

Voice Activator Reflections: Are there times when you let your students see you sweat? If so, when and where? What do you think they learn from that? How can you prevent negative perceptions of anything that you do within your school? Which adult conversations should always take place behind closed doors?

THE INTERVIEW COMMITTEE MIRAGE

It was Miss Jenkins' first year teaching and we were her first class. She was so cool. She is really an awesome teacher. But she was temporary and had to interview for a permanent position. The kids liked her, her teacher friends liked her, so why interview for something that she could just be hired for instead of making her wait and sweat it out? Why bring other teachers in to interview them when we all wanted Miss Jenkins? But a full interview day took place and I saw people coming in to the building with their interview suits on and stuff like that. Not really fair to others if we know who is most likely going to get the job. Don't get me wrong, we don't know if Miss Jenkins had any enemies at our school or someone who wouldn't want to hire her on that huge interview committee, but from what we saw, she was the best and still is. Why do we waste time, money, and energy looking for something that is already under our nose?

—Riley, Grade 9

Miss Jenkins ended up being hired. But Riley still wanted to speak up about her experience. In her eyes, interviews and two long days of interviewing twelve other teachers wasted Riley's time. While she didn't know the intricacies of the adult decisions involved in recruiting and interviewing teachers, she looked at the process and outcome through her own lens and offered up reasonable questions.

She committed healthy treason by pushing back on a process that she felt pulled time, money, resources, and energy away from her school.

When we talked with Riley on her student turf in Detroit, Michigan, Riley took her frustrations about the interview "dog and pony show" to her pen and paper and created her story, which helped her school district reflect on its hiring procedures.

The secrecy of hiring a teacher and the protocols that go with it should never outweigh common sense and open communication. A process that doesn't waste time is best for students and teachers. Riley took the initiative and placed a spotlight on an area that she didn't think worked so well. She wasn't a human resources specialist, but she did provide a student's take on a long-standing policy in her school district, which mirrors many other human resources procedures in schools across the nation.

Examining the Plotlines

Riley's bold analysis got her school officials to start thinking. Her respectful, healthy treason spurred the district to look at improving efficiency and placing student interests above old and outdated policies.

The Student Voice Plotline: "I can't believe I am sitting here listening to all of these nice people interview, and I wonder if they'll feel misled when we end up choosing Miss Jenkins anyway? Why are we doing all of this? I could be getting my stuff done in class right now. Why does hiring have to be like this? Why do we stick to a process we know will waste time, money, and resources, not to mention an entire process that misleads professionals into thinking they have a shot at a job that is most likely going to someone else before they even interview?"

What We Need to Consider: How do we rethink the things we've always done? How do we identify those student voices that will help us analyze what we do in even greater depths? How do we invite students to examine processes that we think are fine and be open to their suggestions? How can we better reflect on what we do and why we do it?

Voice Activator Reflections: It might be possible to recoup lost time during the school day by taking a fresh look at long-standing practices. What are some policies and processes you want to revisit at your school?

NO HELP AFTER SCHOOL?

When your school day is over, is your school a ghost town? Are teachers available to help kids with homework or projects? Before school, do you have students congregating out front, unattended because teachers are not yet required to be on duty? Take a look at a school where teachers breeze in right before the bell rings and walk out at the same time as the students:

> We hang out in front of the school waiting for school to start. My mom has work and always drops me off early. In the morning, we see our teachers come into school just before the bell is about to ring. They are all wearing the same colored shirt and walking in a single line. And then at the end of the day, right when we are leaving the school, the teachers walk single file out of the building and get in their cars to go home. Miss Sherry said something about "work to rule," but I'm not really sure about what that is. But there aren't any teachers in the school before we get there or after school if we need help, except one teacher: Mr. Crowly. I think they leave right away because they are working without a new contract. But who gets the short end of the stick? We do.
>
> **—Adrienne, Grade 4**

Some teachers go into the profession because it is their calling, and to others, it is a job. When teaching becomes a job, every minute off the clock becomes a point of contention. We are not criticizing unions for their "work to rule" as a means to prevent a teacher strike; in fact, we have both been members of teacher unions and administrative unions in the past. What we are criticizing is the message we send to children when adult energies become focused on things other than children. We are not pointing fingers at the union illustrated in this story, but Sean Crowly, a New York teacher, decided as a new teacher and new teacher's union member that he wasn't going to wear the same color shirt as the union, walk in and out of his school in a single file, or refuse to stay after school to help students master his subject. He did not allow the union position about the "work-to-rule" norm of unions standing their ground during times of unrest or contract pursuit that was happening in his district to limit his interactions with students.

Adrienne's narrative was shared with the union leadership of the school after she opened up to her teacher, and although it came across very professionally by Adrienne, we would like to caution readers that students should never be placed in the middle of adult grievances, and we know you would agree. That's why this story is so powerful.

While this was risky to have Sean share Adrienne's letter with union leadership, it didn't backfire, and the union actually changed its position slightly to stay after school for thirty minutes after dismissal if students needed help. This type of healthy treason led to the powerful humanity of the union coming out to support students in order to see them flourish. Such a reflection may have worked well in this school, but again, be careful as to how stories will position children or deal with issues that are out of our hands—as we outlined in Chapter 1. Here, the union was not perceived as insensitive, and adult interests were placed after student interests. This is a powerful example of how the business of schools can bend and accommodate students before any other adult interest. It is a celebration of how union leaders have incredible hearts, and all they needed was a reflective moment about students' perspectives and perceptions about everything going on around them without placing students in the middle of adult grievances.

Examining the Plotlines

Adrienne's emotions and feelings about her teachers and school drove her to open up and tell her story. As a result, her school improved because of her own healthy treason. Take a look at how her plotlines hit the hearts of the union, as the outcome was an absolute victory for both staff and students.

The Student Voice Plotline: "I need help. Can you help me? I know your issues are important, but so are mine, and I'm here at school waiting for you. I need you. Can you please help me with my math? I don't understand it, and I just need to sit with you for a few minutes after school."

What We Need to Consider: How can we remain professional while also doing what's right? How can we stay true to our colleagues and still fight our own battles when necessary? In any field, professional and personal growth are intertwined and they both hinge on being able to admit mistakes and do better. Educators are no different. What are some things you have had second thoughts about or reversed your position on? How can teachers analyze their routines and practices to make sure students are always placed first?

Voice Activator Reflections: In what ways can you push back on the status quo at your school to offer your students more support? Is there anyone you need to apologize to? How can you rethink your school and classroom routines to ensure student needs are a priority?

We must buck up and allow our students to tell us things that we might take the wrong way or become upset about and then label those things as helpful to our growth, not crippling to our egos.

THE NEED TO HAVE POSITIVE PRESS

What is powerful about the **Let Them Speak!** Project is that no one is immune to the reflection students can offer to us individually or as a group. Educators of all kinds—teachers, teacher leaders, principals, superintendents, and school board members—can activate incredible changes when they do not muffle student voice. Take a look at what Abby tells us about her principal, Mr. Robbins, in this next narrative:

> Mr. Robbins is all about looking good. He invites the news and newspaper for the tiniest things. Then he was with some of my friends in a newscast about a picnic we had for a kid who was sick, like some fundraiser thing, and he would barely let the kids say anything on camera. Mr. Robbins talked and talked and talked, and it even looked like he shoved Jessie out of the way with his elbow. I think the news guy was annoyed too. I think they cut off Mr. Robbins. It was hilarious. Anything for the spotlight. Always trying to look good to others. The funny thing is that he's a nice guy, but a terrible principal. We never see him. He's an office beaver—you know, building a dam with furniture so no one can get in.
>
> **—Abby, Grade 5**

Although this story seems kind of funny and silly, Mr. Robbins is a media hog. He thrives on it, thinks his school should be portrayed as superior at all times, and wants to take all of the credit when positive press comes to town. We are not really sure about what drives his behaviors, but it's Abby's perception that Mr. Robbins is fake and takes all of the credit for student and school successes. The other issue is that Abby perceives him as an invisible principal. In her view, he's rarely around. When a principal's visibility decreases, the potential for problems to happen or for achievement to decline increases.

That lack of leadership can be a game changer for both students and staff. The "Wizard of Oz" behind the curtain is ineffective, and Abby knows it.

Abby wrote this narrative in class after sharing her story with us on the playground of her elementary school in Richmond, Virginia, but she never shared it with her school. Abby decided not to speak with Mr. Robbins about her narrative. She struggled to feel comfortable about doing it and didn't want to come across as disrespectful. She also didn't want him to see that she called him a "beaver." In this case, the **Let Them Speak!** Project applauds Abby's decision to not share her narrative. Our main goal was to have students be comfortable with opening up, not clamming up. In this case, the narrative served as something of a diary for Abby instead of an open letter to be shared with an entire staff.

However, Abby agreed to let us share her story in this book because she knew that her real name would not be used and she still wanted to send a message to educators and school leaders across the nation who take credit for anything where credit is not due. Abby wants educators to highlight each other's triumphs as well as student victories. Selfishness and vanity can be seen by students even when we think they aren't looking, and we must allow their voices to help us do better and be better.

Examining the Plotlines

Abby's emotions came through in her narrative, but she was in no way disrespectful throughout the process. She is a great kid with a great heart and when we asked her to talk, she was open and honest. Abby wants her school to focus on student success, not adult media coverage.

The Student Voice Plotline: "I can see that you are not working as a team or building others up. I like to see my teachers and principal working together on issues. We know when there is tension in a room. We know when adults aren't being true to their school or are not feeling the slightest bit of humility. Please showcase student victories or your colleagues' victories, not your own. Why do you want to take all of the credit for the good things that happen at our school? Are you afraid of something? Are you afraid that someone might think that you are not doing a good job? Are you afraid of losing your job? Don't be. You will shine brighter when you shine the light on others."

What We Need to Consider: How can we showcase our school's or students' success without taking all the credit ourselves? What message should we send to students about recognition for hard work? How can educators move their schools forward without leaving anyone behind?

Voice Activator Reflections: How can we showcase student victories and silence our own desires to be noticed as the expert?

MY COUNSELOR ONLY KNOWS ME WHEN TRAGEDY STRIKES

One of the many lessons that the **Let Them Speak!** Project taught us when we talked with students was that we need to encourage our students to use their voices even when things are good. We need to have gratitude for everything amazing that is happening because if we only step up to the plate when things go wrong, we could be perceived as educators who are only part-time caretakers. Full-time love is a requirement for every educator in every classroom in every school. Ronny's story reminds us of that in a very dramatic way:

> My father died a couple of weeks ago. I've been going to this school since sixth grade. I never met my counselor until two weeks ago. She wanted to check in with me

because my dad died, and my mom called to see if I could talk to someone. I don't want to talk to a stranger. I mean no disrespect to my counselor, but I don't know anything about her. Sure, I know what she looks like because I've been here for so long—but not even a "hello." Not sure if she would know my name if I walked by her. And if my mom hadn't called, she would never have known that my dad died, anyway. I'm not trying to be rude or anything, but why does something big have to happen in my life for my counselor to chat with me?

—Ronny, Grade 8

Ronny's story didn't hurt his counselor's feelings. It didn't hurt his teacher's feelings or his principal's feelings, either. His narrative did help the local school board to reduce the school counselors' caseloads by adding two additional full-time counselors to each middle school in the district. This move was coupled with an intense mentor program where all of the students would meet with their counselor once a month to go over academics, issues, or just laugh and get to know one another.

This change was monumental. Student voice led Ronny's school to intentionally support children when times are good and when times are bad. This story transformed a school culture—all because Ronny spoke up, and someone listened.

Examining the Plotlines

Ronny activated the narrative process because we asked him to share his voice. He pointed out a system flaw with how students were (or were not) being serviced. He felt like his counselor was a complete stranger to him and he was right. There was something wrong with the system of offering guidance to children in Ronny's own backyard, and his narrative will open our eyes to possible similar situations that exist in our own systems.

The Student Voice Plotline: "Am I important to you each day, or only when tragedy strikes? Will you take care of me each day, or just when someone tells you I need help? Will you be present for my victories and good news, or just my pitfalls and mistakes?"

What We Need to Consider: In what ways do we inadvertently forget about our students when there is so much to do each day? How can teachers maximize what they do well for students and minimize the things that don't really matter? How can school leaders help their educators be more effective in the lives of their students or activate proactive plans that celebrate victories, rather than only focus on foibles or tragedies?

Voice Activator Reflections: So many times, we enter our school buildings with the intent of altering students' behaviors when it's actually *our* behaviors that need to change. What can you do to check in with your students more frequently than you already do? What types of feedback can you gather that would help you care for your students in new ways? What can you do to show your students support when times are good and bad?

When we ask our students the right questions, we will get real answers. We must listen to our clients attentively and be willing to assimilate their feedback no matter how we want to initially respond. One thing we know for certain is that we have the power to use their stories to reflect on what we do each day to become better at what we ultimately do for our students.

Chapter 3
Instructional Insanity

One or two bad teachers is a problem with the teachers. A school with many bad teachers is a problem of leadership.

—Andy Hargreaves

So much of what we do is focused on instruction. From learning targets to depth of knowledge, from deconstructing the standards to planning for misconceptions, it is all part of the system of planning instruction. We watch webinars on instructional pedagogy, read books to amplify our professional planning and instruction, and participate in countless hours of professional development to better ourselves for our students. We want to stay current, fresh, and invigorated in the newest methods of teaching and learning so our students do not lose faith in us.

We ooze teaching, learning, and leading. At the same time, we're missing some vital data: our students' thoughts and feelings about what we do with them in class. What could *they* tell us about our instruction that would be helpful? What could *they* share that would help us improve? Can we alter our egos and realize that with student feedback, voice, and choice, our lessons can get better even if we hold a master's degree and our students don't? What if they know as much, if not more, about how *they* learn than we do? We mean no disrespect with this idea, and we recognize the hard work and advanced degrees of countless teachers across the country. But we firmly believe students hold essential information that could help ease their anxieties—as well as pressures on teachers—during the learning process. The key is making a commitment to extracting that information.

Students must be granted permission and given time to share their thoughts about instructional styles, specific lessons, and learning environments. They must be allowed to reveal what they like, dislike, don't understand, or find frustrating. While carrying out the fieldwork for this book, we were fortunate enough to have many students open up to us about the daily instruction that they receive.

Up to now, we focused heavily on relationships, the power of establishing good ones, and not having our students see us model terrible behaviors. We talked about their perceptions about *us*— what they see *us* do, what they see *us* not doing, and everything in between. In this chapter, you will find that many of the things that drive teachers nuts also drive students nuts! What we might think is an awesome philosophy, lesson, or policy in our classroom isn't doing anything to aid in our students' learning. Here are a few student narratives about classroom instruction:

GRADING BEHAVIOR

We all have heard it before: Students struggle with grades. Sometimes things become even more complicated as they are disengaged, misguided, withdrawn, or just simply defiant about school. There are teachers out there who pick up on this, wish to run a smooth class, and not have many headaches at the end of the day. Then there are teachers who use grades as a behavior-management tool, and this practice upsets lots of students! Teresa, a fifth grader, had this to say about her school's grading practices:

> I do really well on my tests, mostly hand in my homework assignments, and really try hard to stay after school when I can to make up any missed work. I think my average would be like eighty-five percent if it wasn't for my "behavior." I don't do anything bad in class. It's just, well, you know, sometimes I like to talk and then I get hit with the behavior points at the end of the quarter. My grade drops down to, like, a seventy-nine percent or an eighty percent, if I'm lucky. I don't think it's fair—giving kids' grades on their behavior. Raymond barely says anything in class and he got a 104 percent in math class last quarter. He pulled extra credit because of his good behavior? And I talk a little bit here and there and get crushed? It's not fair. It's really not fair at all.
>
> **—Teresa, Grade 5**

For a fifth grader, this is pretty deep. Teresa knows what inequity looks like. She knows, without exactly articulating it, what inequity is. Teresa shared her story while hanging out with her friends on the chewed-up blacktop basketball court near her small community school just outside of Harrisburg, Pennsylvania. Her teacher, Erin Morris, was there too and listened to what students had to say about how they were graded. Afterward, she took her students back to class and asked them to write down their thoughts. For some of the students, behavior points were freebies and they liked the way they were graded. They weren't as inclined to complain about the grading process. Why would they speak up when their talkative friends and the disengaged students, who were already labeled as troublemakers, could take all the heat? We asked some of Teresa's friends that question, and some of the "well-behaved students," who racked up points for complying, knew exactly what we were challenging them to consider: one student's decision to speak up might be ruining the party. For other students, the entire policy of grading behavior was a slap in the face.

This plotline tells us an awful lot about our beliefs and practices about grading and what we do for students, try to do for students, or think will help students. As a result of this story from the basketball court, Erin and many other teachers reconsidered how they incorporate behavior into their students' overall grades—those grades that should be based on mastery of standards, deep work, effort, and growth from one point to another. They decided their students should be able to work toward each of those goals without being penalized for talking out of turn or wiggling around in their chairs just because they were really bored out of their minds. After all, the lack of student engagement, motivation, and fun in learning was the root of the problem. Leveling the playing field and not penalizing students for noncompliant behaviors was really the topic at hand.

Examining the Plotlines

Even if some students liked the freebie behavior points, and others hated them, what is interesting to note is how everyone was really talking about compliance in the classroom and how to be forced, through grades, to not bother others. When the students in Teresa's class bothered others, it was because they were bored out of their minds. At the end of the day, is that equitable proof of learning?

The Student Voice Plotline: "I don't think it's fair to take points away from me because I'm not a perfectly behaved student. Maybe

Imagine your spouse or mother grading your moodiness, anger, forgetfulness, or chattiness within your marriage or while growing up. If that were the case, we would all be F students! So why do we call out our students' humanness by assigning them a big, fat capital letter?

you can understand that sometimes I'm just antsy and don't like the lesson or subject. Other times, I'm just plain bored. I'm not a bad student or a bad kid. Will you please loosen up and give us activities where we can talk or at least move around the room? Can you teach me without hurting my grade? I know the content and do the work, so why do you have to punish me for it?"

What We Need to Consider: In what ways can we reconsider grading and behavior management in our classrooms? What are some new ways to allow kids the breathing room they need, but also keep them academically focused?

Voice Activator Reflections: Are there practices in our craft that are punitive rather than supportive of a positive growth mindset? How can we ensure equity for all? Is there anything you currently do that works against student learning? How do you allow your students to demonstrate mastery of a standard beyond completing worksheets and assignments?

MINUS TEN POINTS FOR NOT HAVING SCHOOL SUPPLIES

This next issue might seem a little picky and a little ridiculous, but it creates real anxiety for many students—and we wouldn't have known about it without asking them. Like grading classroom behavior, grading students on whether they bring in all the correct school supplies is another good example of instructional insanity. As Owen, a candid and plainspoken sixth grader, explains, the tediousness of having to comply with silly school supply rules drives him—and his mom—absolutely nuts! His narrative is a good reminder that student compliance with school rules isn't always within their control. Here's what Owen had to say:

I gotta buy tissues and Clorox wipes as part of my school supplies? My mom goes nuts when she sees those things on the supply list and then refuses to buy them. Then I go in to school and get my name written down on the board because I'm still supposed to bring in tissues. I told my teacher that my mom flipped out and won't buy them for me, but I'm the one who gets into trouble? When I think it's just at the start of the year that I have to buy these bogus school supplies, it creeps up on me when I start a new special area class like art or technology maybe halfway through the year. It's like there is a Clorox wipes conspiracy out there to get me. I didn't even tell my mom about the ones I had to buy last week because I didn't want to hear about it again. I asked my friend, Danielle, to give me one of her two canisters of wipes, and she did— which was really nice, but then we both got a look from our teacher for not having two canisters each. I felt bad for Danielle because she was being so nice about help-ing me only to find out that she got points taken off for not having all of her school supplies, either. Crazy. Really crazy. Since when are students supposed to buy all this stuff? Whatever happened to just paper, pencils, pens, and some folders?

—Owen, Grade 6

Maybe Owen makes a great point. Maybe teachers become so focused on the lack of resources that we end up transferring more and more of the burden to students and their families. Teachers mean well. They want clean classrooms, disinfected classrooms. Their goal is to minimize illness and germs and who doesn't want that? But the reality is most school budgets are running on fumes, and teach-ers barely scrape by with low wages spread across 180 days of work. To some, this might seem like a minor issue, but when it's tied to grading and not losing points—and a student's mom flat-out refuses to buy certain supplies—it could grow into a larger problem. For Owen, there's clearly a level of anxiety that shouldn't be ignored. He wanted to write about his feelings on this topic so he could be heard! We imagine there are countless educators laughing as they read this because it's a common scenario that plays out at the start of every year in schools across the country: school supplies preparedness!

Examining the Plotlines

Sometimes, what we think might be a silly issue causes our students incredible anxiety. That anxiety can often be transformed into having ill feelings about any given topic or issue on any given day.

The Student Voice Plotline: "I want to be graded on what matters, not nonsense. I just started school, and my name is already on the board."

What We Need to Consider: In what ways do we grade or penalize students for things beyond academic achievement and mastery of standards? What are some grading policies you would like to revisit in your own school? Should we be growth oriented? What does growth really look like? What does achievement look like? These are the questions that will keep pushing educators' understanding about student assessment and grading into new horizons dedicated to problem-based learning (PBL), real-world relevance, and authentic learning in its most distilled form, not a quasi, sort-of accumulation of points that we feel we need to award students when they comply with what we want.

Voice Activator Reflections: How can you teach responsibility and still promote generosity with a positive approach? In what manner or under what conditions is it appropriate to require your students to bring in supplies? Are there any other seemingly minor

To be graded and penalized for others' actions (or inactivity) won't teach our students anything. It is like dishing out one hundred dollars to a doctor who writes you a prescription for a placebo sugar pill that won't heal anything.

issues in your classroom that chip away at relationships, which can then chip away at a student's positive attitude or success?

GROUP WORK AND COOPERATIVE LEARNING THAT PENALIZES STUDENTS

Student voices can rejuvenate what we do, how we do it, and better yet, why we do it. Think about cooperative learning and group work. Enter a student who works hard within a group. Enter the "perceived slacker" who couldn't care less, not because he or she is a bad kid, but because he or she couldn't care less about something that doesn't excite them. We can all remember working on group projects—in grade school, college, and even the workplace—and having to deal with that one person who didn't pull his or her weight. This made us wonder about how group work or cooperative learning is conceived in our classrooms. How do teachers ensure functional groups? How do they maximize student learning and teach students how to develop positive working relationships—a skill that is necessary throughout their lives? Take a look at what one nine-year-old said about group work at her school:

> Group work. I hate group work. We are supposed to learn how to work together, but Roger never does anything in our group. Then, we get a group grade and my teacher tells me that we all have to figure it out and work together. Figure what out? Try to convince someone to do their part when they won't even listen to us? It gets worse. We had to grade one another (secretly) with this rating sheet of criteria that we all had to hand in to our teacher. When we got our group grade back, we received a seventy percent! I worked my tail off and so did Samantha, and Roger just sat there and brought our group grade down

because he didn't do the science diagrams like he was supposed to. I swear, in the future if we ever have to do group work, I'm doing it all myself. That's what we learn, I guess: to just "work it out"—but for what? A low grade?
—Sophia, Grade 4

After we had an opportunity to talk with Sarah, Mrs. Langston asked Sophia to write down what she thought could or should be done to deal with dysfunctional group behavior. Sophia had us in stitches when we spoke to her. She was a firecracker. She practiced healthy treason with a twist, that's for sure!

But, what if Sophia is right? What if there is an entire generation of students out there who feel the same way about group work? Is it right when group work is handled in a punitive way by any teacher who takes a *laissez-faire* approach to assigning groups and then demands that the students just "figure it out" on their own? Teachers should be intentional about grouping students and should have a specific reason why they choose to assign groups. Are we supporting negligent behaviors by not addressing students' concerns about their own learning? Accountability for managing group work, in this instance, turned toxic because students were responsible for managing each other, and if it didn't work out, they would be penalized.

Examining the Plotlines

Solutions for servicing students in the best possible way that we can will sometimes become cloudy for both teachers and students. To get a sense of the cloudiness, we need someone to tell us that it is, indeed, going to rain.

The Student Voice Plotline: "I am my own person who can do my own work. Group work is sometimes good and sometimes bad based on someone else either interested or disinterested. I like the collaboration and I like the projects because they keep the class from being boring. But my grade shouldn't suffer because of someone else in the group. While I know that not everyone will always do their fair share, should their individual choices bring down my grade-point average and success here in school? I feel like I am being punished for someone else's lack of motivation, even when I was 100% invested in the work that needed to get done."

What We Need to Consider: In what ways can we be understanding when helping students work with one another versus making things difficult or uncomfortable? How can we hold individuals accountable for their contributions to group work rather than penalizing the entire team of students?

Voice Activator Reflections: What more do you feel you need to know to implement powerful collaborative learning in your classroom? How can you ensure equity for all students when the playing field is not level? Does teaching your students responsibility come before helping them learn? What criteria should be used to effectively implement cooperative learning?

The capacity to learn is a gift; the ability to learn is a skill; the willingness to learn is a choice.

–Brian Herbert

TEACHING LITERATURE THAT KIDS CAN'T STAND

Sometimes kids despise what you love—even the literature you could spend hours discussing. Out on the sports field, Johnny, a seventh-grade student, sat with us and his teacher, Tori Greenburg, in their student council lounge just off the side entrance to their cafeteria. Tori asked students about what they had read together in her class that year. Take a look at what Johnny said:

> I've never hated *Where the Red Fern Grows* as much as I do when I think back to having to read it last month. The thought of it still makes me sick. I'm not a teacher or anything, so I'm sure I will get a teacher answer and response as to why teaching novels (or teaching this novel) to a whole class is important in education, but I wanted to stick a pin in my eye while reading this book. I hated it. Did I say that already? It wasn't fun, funny, or interesting at all, but we had to read it every night for like a month until we took a test and were done with it—until final-exam time when we reviewed how this book would help us out in terms of the themes of conflict, coming of age, and all that literary analysis mumbo-jumbo. Why are we forced to read three novels a year with the entire class? Why is *Where the Red Fern Grows* taught all over the place? My friends who go to school in another district have to read it too. I think the book was like from a long time ago, too. Why didn't the author just use the word "dogs" instead of "pups?" It drove me crazy. Who determined that this book was good for all seventh graders, anyway? How did this book get all these awards? I'm not even a dog person. I like cats better and have three of them.
>
> **—Johnny, Grade 7**

Teachers have taught literature as part of a whole-class activity and forum for years on end, and Johnny is quite right: *Where the Red Fern Grows* is considered a classic. It was a Newbery Medal winner and a Printz Honor Book. Teachers across the globe use this book as part of their curriculum, but Johnny makes a really good point. How does a book achieve international status? Why does a whole class have to study the same book in a communal fashion for more than a month; in fact, this book study went on for longer than that!

We are not mocking whole-group literature instruction, but we are pushing back on one thing: the decision to design a unit around a book that might have limited appeal among students, even if adults have highly acclaimed it to be an award winner is worth analyzing in terms of student voice!

Examining the Plotlines

Reading something together as a class is not an enemy practice. Reading something for a really long time and making a decision to select all the literature for students or all of the books or resources for students to consume should be looked at very closely.

The Student Voice Plotline: "Why do I have to read what you want me to read, especially when I don't enjoy reading it? Why do I have to read what the rest of the class is reading? I'm not a teacher and I'm sure you will tell me why whole-class novels are important, but when we hate a text, there really is no turning back. Why is that? Can't I still learn without reading that book?"

What We Need to Consider: In what ways are we so stuck in our practices that we fail to recognize what our students really want, both instructionally and emotionally?

Voice Activator Reflections: Under what circumstance is it necessary for everybody to read what you picked out? How could you give your students a choice and still ensure they are mastering a learning standard? How do you foster a love of reading in your classroom and school? Do you want your students to forever remember a book they hated, or remember reading strategies they can carry with them for comprehension and thematic reflection? How do you coordinate reading and writing instruction in your classroom? In what ways can you gauge reading interest in new and formative ways?

ASK STUDENTS WHAT THEY LIKE TO READ

Let's take Johnny's narrative from above and go one step further. Check out this story that was shared with us on the playground of an elementary school in Akron, Ohio:

> I like male characters. They are real. They are exciting. They bring suspense to the books we have to read. Without these books, I would be kinda bored with the same old stereotypical female main character in the novels that my teachers think that I want to read. The fact is: I only want to read about male characters. More action. More stuff going on and not girly stuff, either. I just like the topics and characters better. They are so funny. I even remember reading *Galaxy Zack* books instead of *Amelia Bedelia* when I was in second grade.
>
> **—Andrea, Grade 5**

As a result of this narrative, Dean Matthewson, a fourth-grade teacher, decided to really listen and figure out why his male students did poorly on a literature test about Alexander Keys' *The Forgotten Door* while his female students did quite well. So he gave a brief four-question survey about what his students liked or didn't like about their in-class literature studies and essay "tests" that went along with the content. The results were as follows:

1. Almost eighty percent of the female students liked reading literature with a male the protagonist.
2. About fifteen percent of male students were okay with *The Forgotten Door* but didn't necessarily attribute their success or lack of success on the test to the protagonist being male.

According to the survey, female students received higher grades on the essay test than the male students by a 15:1 ratio. The survey revealed that female students would rather read about an exciting male protagonist than a boring or exciting female protagonist. This gave Dean Matthewson and his ELA department an opportunity to analyze texts, make new recommendations for what to purchase, and canvass students earlier in the school year about what they wanted to read.

It assisted Dean's principal in making better purchasing decisions based on literature recommendations from the teachers, who had a better understanding of their students' preferences, likes, and dislikes.

Examining the Plotlines

What we purchase, what we select, and what we showcase for student learning has deeper decision-making biases than we can see. There is always more to the story of why students do something very well or not very well and student voice can reveal those nuances.

The Student Voice Plotline: "I have different tastes that you don't know about. You don't realize what I really enjoy in class. Just because I am a female doesn't mean that I like female stereotypes."

What We Need to Consider: In what ways can we think about how to construct versus deconstruct our students' interest in literature and the protagonists who speak to them? How can we teach literature with a fresh approach and go beyond the traditional status quo nature of what is being taught and why we teach it? All across the nation, curriculum committees meet to make decisions about what students should learn and how we should align our curriculum to standards-based learning. Why do we, as adults, shoulder the burden of creating curriculum and content without any student input?

Voice Activator Reflections: What can you ask students about their courses before and after you deliver instruction? How can we informally seek student voices to help us construct our curriculum?

Do you and your colleagues create curriculum without student input? Do you consider curriculum alignment to be an adult task or an adult-and-student task? Why? What will you do differently this year in order to prepare for next year?

THE HORSESHOE TABLE IN THE BACK

As educators, we always aim for the best possible lesson plan right off the bat. Along the way, we check to make sure everyone understands the content and when we have students who don't, we might meet them at the table in the back of the classroom. This is a common practice. Additional time and additional practice is often a school-wide and district-wide expectation for RtI strategies. But not everyone likes being summoned to the back table—a practice that often starts as early as pre-kindergarten and kindergarten. Amy Sandoval, a kindergarten teacher in Huntsville, Alabama, sat alongside several students on the grass outside her classroom window because she wanted to ask them about learning math. Here is what she found out:

> I live at the back table. We do math on the carpet. Every time [Miss Sandoval] calls me to the back table to do it again. The same way over and over. I still don't get it. I don't get it at the carpet or the back table. Sometimes I just say I get it so I can go do centers with the other kids.
> **—Jose, Kindergarten**

> I like the back table because I get to be with my teacher. We just do the same lesson again, though. I try hard, but I still don't get it. It doesn't matter because I get to be with Miss Sandoval and she pays attention to me. But I don't like math too much.
> **—Sherry, Kindergarten**

Every teacher understands that every student might not learn something the first time. Most teachers understand and embrace the developmental differences of being a kid. Many schools are groomed to look at data and follow a rigorous RtI plan for instructional interventions to occur in almost any subject area. We know how to check for understanding and reteach those kids again. But Jose and Sherry provided insights into how Miss Sandoval was facilitating her reteach lessons, not what the content was or what math concept they were learning. They helped her realize that she was just doing the same lesson slower and louder, not differently in terms of delivery or strategies.

For some kids, modeling and direct, explicit instruction works. Other kids might require a different strategy or a kinesthetic approach. The responses of Jose and Sherry are quite brilliant on many levels. Their voices shed light on their teacher's craft and elicited massive changes to her approach and instructional delivery. The improvements resulted in major academic gains for both Jose and Sherry and maybe even other students who had to visit the table in the back of the room at some point during their school year.

Examining the Plotlines

Students need something more than repetition, isolation, or removal. They need validation and autonomy to charter their own courses. We can guide students, coach them, model for them, and then hand over the torch to let them run wild with all that excites them.

The Student Voice Plotline: "I like the back table. I want to learn what you teach, but my brain doesn't hear it right. When you teach it to me the same way again, I still don't get it. Can you show me a different way?"

What We Need to Consider: Checking for student understanding during each lesson is a powerful practice. Providing students an opportunity to give it another try at the back table is even more powerful. What specific learning style does each student prefer? How can you plan to teach each lesson a different way using a different modality than the first time?

Voice Activator Reflections: What do you consider essential elements for a reteach lesson? How can you teach the lesson differently and more concretely than you did for the whole class? How can you vary your instruction to make it stick for each child?

At the juncture where relationships and instruction intersect, there is an additional school spirit and school facet of completing the total school program, and that includes school-wide or district-wide programming. Chapter 4 will explore two different kinds of programs—antibullying and community service—in schools that we visited. We examine how student voice can enhance already established school programs—even programs that are perceived to be doing the right things and running like well-oiled machines. The operative word here is "perceived." When you have successfully implemented a program year to year without any pushback or issues, it could be assumed that things are fine. Sometimes reality is much different when we *Let Them Speak!*

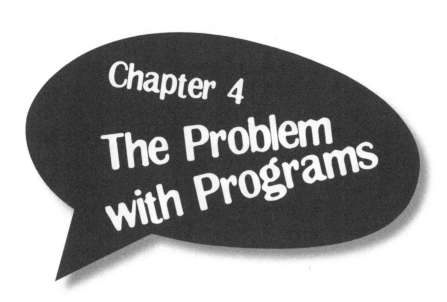

Chapter 4
The Problem
with Programs

The beauty of empowering others is that your own power is not diminished in the process.

—Barbara Coloroso

The more we listened to our clients, the more it became clear we might be doing some things the wrong way. During one of the *Let Them Speak!* Project turf sessions, we were stopped dead in our tracks by a discussion about bullying. We all believe school should be a safe, risk-free learning environment, and most schools now lead some sort of antibullying initiative. Programming is established. Policies are set. Students are trained. Zero tolerance is expected. Speakers are invited to share their experiences about bullying, often relaying horrific events. It's almost as if some educators think kids can be scared into not bullying others.

Programs of this nature sound good, and we mean well. But what if these antibullying efforts are missing the mark in ways that no one is talking about or even realizes? Antibullying programs often do not illustrate the side effects of such protective, well-intended programming structures. We get our prescriptions from the drug store with pamphlets of information about side effects, yet we don't stop in our tracks before implementing school- or district-wide programming and question it every step of the way before unveiling what we believe are well-calculated programs that will protect all children. You are probably wondering what could be so wrong about something that seems so right, and even though this entire book is not at all about a "right versus wrong" approach, it is about opening up new transformations of what we can do even better than we are already doing. We just need to ask our students what they think about what we work on or create for our students day in and day out.

BULLYING, DISTILLED

Do we place too much pressure on our students? Do we ask children to do too much while they are in school trying to learn reading, writing, and arithmetic, only to find out that they don't really want to be asked to solve the world's problems? We believe that students who face injustice can and will step up to stomp out bullying, but maybe we focus too much on programs that highlight upstanders and bystanders who must step up to eradicate bullying. Let us explain.

During our fieldwork, we learned more about antibullying campaigns than any book ever written about bullying could provide. We don't mean to sound arrogant about our findings. We are just so blown away by some of the student voices we activated on a topic that is so widely known to schools. Thanks to student voice, we now have a new lens through which to view antibullying programs across the nation. We found that a great deal of the antibullying programming out there is comfortable for adults, but for children, that same programming can include scary requests, urgent demands, and extreme pressures and anxieties.

Bullying is everywhere. We might define bullying as repeated, aggressive, and intentional use of words and actions that cause distress and compromise well-being. It's a targeted and repeated behavior that exists in the locker room, on the playground, in the workplace, and even in politics. Children make fun of anything that they can get their hands on, but they learn these behaviors from adults. Bullying exists in every school and in almost every social setting in existence.

So, what did we do? We asked students what they thought about bullying and their schools' efforts to fight it, and here is what one particular student summed up for dozens and dozens of other students who felt the same way! Take a look at what Jerry, a ninth grader, told us:

> I hated Thursdays. My palms would get sweaty and my heart would race. I constantly looked at the doorway listening for the cadence of his walk, and the clink of his keys against the clipboard as Coach Randolph walked into the PE class during my last period. I tried telling him that I was being harassed relentlessly by the other kids about my height. It happened the most in PE.
>
> **—Jerry, Grade 9**

Jerry shared his story while sitting in the student lounge at his high school in Bloomington, Indiana. He wanted help, but standing up to other students was scary. We captured the narrative of our conversation because we felt so compelled to share this information with his administrator, and especially Coach Randolph. We scheduled a meeting with Principal Ross Galvin the following morning and shared Jerry's narrative. Principal Galvin ran his fingers around the edge of the paper, then put his index finger to his lips with a look of deep thought. Slowly he sat up tall and shared that he was appreciative of the information and that he would take care of things. He thanked us, shook our hands, and walked us out.

Not knowing what this really meant, we were somewhat fearful of betraying Jerry's trust. We hadn't shared Jerry's name, but if Principal Galvin talked to Coach Randolph, he could easily track it back to Jerry if he remembered the conversation. About two weeks passed and we received a call from Principal Galvin. He said he spent a week just observing student transition times to and from PE and he noticed that the freshman students were clustered by social groups. One particular group often pointed, whispered, and laughed at other students.

Principal Galvin had witnessed this social dynamic with his own eyes. He knew it needed to be addressed but also wanted to empower the students with a solution. Particularly, he wanted to impact the group causing the issue. During study hall the next day, Principal Galvin called up this group of seven boys to the office conference room. He shared with them that there was a bullying problem among the seniors in their school and that he wanted to bring in a team of freshman to get some ideas for possible solutions. Principal Galvin made up a few examples about how it made students feel and how their grades suffered. Then, he asked them for advice on how the school should handle this type of situation. They spent the next twenty minutes brainstorming ideas from an infraction card with consequences to having a meeting with a counselor or a phone call home. You could tell the freshman were playing along but deep down were fearful that they had been caught red-handed.

Finally, one of the biggest boys in the room leaned forward with his elbows on the table and said, "Maybe they need to know what it really feels like and then they would stop doing it." While pacing around the room, Principal Galvin said, "Tell me more." The same student replied, "Maybe sometimes kids are just being kids trying to look cool, but they don't really realize that it is so hurtful."

After another fifteen minutes of discussion, this group of bullies came to a consensus for stopping the very behaviors they had been engaging in. Principal Galvin shared with us that they would have a Google survey reporting system available for any student to submit a formal complaint that would be received by the school counselor. There would be dropdowns on the survey noting whether they wanted someone to take action and investigate, or if it was something they wanted the administrators to be aware of.

Our programming often places a high priority on asking children and teenagers to report abuse when they see it or to tell an adult when something is wrong. Reporting is necessary, but reporting with fear of retribution is frightening for students, and even worse, overlooked or discounted.

STOP ASKING ME TO SOLVE THE WORLD'S PROBLEMS

Many educators work hard to create schools full of activists— students who will stand up for what is right—but that expectation can cause some of them incredible anxiety. Sometimes we look to students to stand up and fight for causes we think they should want to join, but our good intentions are pushing some students into uncomfortable situations.

Kathy Jenkins, a sixth-grade ELA teacher in Little Rock, Arkansas, gathered some of her students on beanbag chairs in the foyer of their school to talk about bullying. She simply asked her students to share what upset them. Sixth grader Leslie's story, which

If kids come to us from strong, heathy, functioning families, it makes our job easier. If they do not come to us from strong, healthy, functioning families, it makes our job more important.

—Barbara Coloroso

later became a written narrative that was shared with her principal, was one of the reasons we wrote this chapter. Here is her account:

> We are supposed to stand up to bullying. It's a school initiative. You know—be an active bystander, they call it. We are supposed to be upstanders—taking action ourselves to stomp out bullying. But no one asks us what we really feel about all of this. I want to help my friends or classmates, but I have my own problems too. It's hard being a kid, sometimes, and I get some anxiety over the whole thing. But the school program is what it is. Led by my principal and teachers. They tell us it is what we have to do as good classmates. Good citizens. But sometimes, it's just overkill. I want to learn about literature and art. I get up in the morning to learn. Schools do so much other stuff that by the end of the day, I swear, I only had a couple hours of academic work. Why is our day packed with so much other stuff that I end up going home with hours of homework because I was told to sit through a character-education workshop about respect and how we shouldn't bully others?
>
> **—Leslie, Grade 6**

After reading Leslie's narrative, Kathy and her fellow teachers and administrators examined what they were doing and pulled back on placing such a strong emphasis on student-led antibullying programs. With the intent of making students more comfortable and not infringing on academic instruction, the school allowed students who were interested in being upstanders to volunteer for its antibullying training programs. That one change brought a great deal of relief to many children who thought they had to eradicate the problem of bullying all on their own.

Examining Plotlines

Sometimes we inadvertently have negative impacts on some students when we don't mean anyone any harm. While programming aims to mean well, there are plotlines we might be unaware of until we ask our students to provide input and insights on anything and everything that we do in our schools.

The Student Voice Plotline: "I have fears and anxieties when asked to do something outside my comfort zone. I know when something is wrong, and I want to help others, but I get scared and don't want my teachers to think that I am condoning terrible behaviors when I don't do something. I don't want to be the target of bullying by standing up to it. I'm not chicken; I'm just me, and I feel so much pressure to be a part of what the school is telling me I need to do."

What We Need to Consider: In what ways can we be more sensitive when designing our school-wide programming in any area? Can we solicit feedback and insights from our students in order to find hidden plotlines that we might not be aware of?

Voice Activator Reflections: What existing programs in your school have resulted in unintended consequences for students? How did you and other educators respond? Have you asked students what they think about the programs that currently exist in your school or ones that you are thinking about setting up?

Take a look at one other viewpoint about antibullying efforts in a school in Buffalo, New York. Samantha, a seventh grader, provided some amazing insights when we sat with her on the bleachers after track and field practice:

> I don't get bullying. I really don't. It is part of life. It's not right, but it's part of life. And, I'm expected to solve the world's problems and save our school from bullying. We sign antibullying pledges, talk about bullying every

single day, it seems, but kids still do it. We participate in an antibullying day. We march around the school with flags. It is so weird. It's like the assemblies create more problems for us kids. Does anyone ever wonder if those assemblies actually work? I heard they spent $2,000 on a guy who was bullied as a kid to come in and speak to all of us. One day of antibullying? Show kindness to someone for one day? More marching around? A food drive? A pledge drive that we have to go around looking for money to donate to the food pantry? And kids still poke fun at other kids. Can't I just go to class and learn? But if I speak up, I will look like the jerk. Like I condone bullying or something. I bet years ago when my teachers were in school, they had bullying too. It will never go away, but my principal runs these marches and assemblies about bullying. And we have to sit there and not say a word. They don't ask us anything about bullying and what we think we should do to try and stop it. I saw Mikey getting in trouble during an assembly because he was making fun of Trisha. It was, like, so ironic. If I could tell my principal one thing it would be: Stop making a big issue of every little thing. It shines a spotlight on the problem more than you think.

—Samantha, Grade 7

Samantha offers a bold look at antibullying efforts, but opens up to us about her opinion in order to help adults look at how repetition of school-wide expectations does little to nothing for stomping out bullying. While Samantha doesn't offer suggestions to fix this problem, she does, in fact, provide insights that overdoing a message actually increases misbehavior about the message. Increasing programming counteracts the good intentions and becomes stale with the students that Samantha actually sees misbehaving even more when a spotlight is placed on problems, not solutions.

Examining Plotlines

In this particular case (and we must stress that this is just one case at one school), the more students are told to not do something or to stop doing something, the more misbehaviors take place. Adults are perceived as broken records, and programming that costs a lot of money can still lead to minimal progress.

The Student Voice Plotline: "Sometimes the more emphasis and energy that we give to something creates a reverse effect. It's like we are paying too much attention to something instead of addressing the situations as they come up. I don't want to be bullied, I really don't. I'm not going to be a bully, either. But the reality is that we are more uncomfortable than the actual bullies who go through the school-wide program. It makes us bigger targets rather than really changing the behavior of the offenders. It is so backwards. Do we have it all wrong?"

What We Need to Consider: Can we reflect on how we might be inadvertently impacting our students in negative ways more than we are actually helping them?

Voice Activator Reflections: How do you get feedback from students about all of your assemblies, program activities, and fund-raising at your school? What works? What doesn't work? What is cool? What is dreaded? What doesn't seem genuine? What do they like? How might that feedback affect future events or activities? Can we measure the success of a program by asking students what they think worked?

THE SIDE EFFECTS OF LABELING

We've all seen it before, and many students are actually quite angry about it. If students make a mistake, bully another child, or misbehave more regularly than one might expect, they are often labeled as troublemakers. These students are then more likely to dis-trust schools—and individual educators—when the entire system is designed to help all students flourish.

Alanna is a fifth grader in St. Paul, Minnesota who is familiar with some of those labels, and she goes through great lengths to share with us how they make her feel:

> I guess I'm a bully. At least, that's what my counselor at school tells me. I get sent down to the office for picking on Lila, and then no one really knows that Lila's brother beat my brother up last week, and when I tell my counselor, she tells me that my brother's school should handle that. But that's my brother. And when Lila flaps her mouth, I tell her I'm gonna close it shut for her. But I'm the bully. So then the more my counselor thinks I'm a bully, I get blamed for stuff I don't even do. It's like they have a radar set up on me, and when I'm nowhere in sight, they still blame me. Gillie even laughed right in my face when she came back from the principal's office, telling him something that I didn't even do. And they get away with it. Shouldn't we be innocent until proven guilty? They take a "good kid's" word for everything, and if someone gets into trouble, they are, forever, a liar. That's not fair. That's not justice. But I get so mad about being blamed for nothing that I talk back and then I get into trouble for talking back.
>
> **—Alanna, Grade 5**

Students don't always mean to cause harm. They have reasons for their behaviors, and most of those reasons are going to be judged by an adult in some capacity. Sometimes adults don't think about students' reasons as "good enough." Sometimes they assume, incor-rectly, a student's reason for acting out and don't give the student the benefit of the doubt or a chance to fully explain their behavior.

The adult labels the student and their behaviors unfairly follow them throughout their school career.

Be diligent in believing that what we do in the classroom could possibly echo for a lifetime in the heart of a student.

−Robert John Meehan

Examining Plotlines

Accessing student voice is an intense journey. It is not always easy. It can be messy, challenging, but incredibly rewarding at the same time. When we fail to access student voice, blame does not have to be placed on the adults. Yet, can we ask ourselves why we didn't activate student voice in something we are working on or doing in the first place? Can we be honest with ourselves about why we don't want to get messy? Can we look at the root causes of what makes our students tick, gain a better understanding of how we can help, and then build up even more sensitive school environments that our students will cherish alongside us?

The Student Voice Plotline: "Sometimes I have reasons for doing something—reasons that adults can't understand unless they think back to when they were a child and maybe take the time to talk to me. Ask me. See if I'm doing something I don't even realize I'm doing, or just take the time to look me in the eyes and make me feel better about myself even if I mess up. I'm going to mess up. I'm a kid."

What We Need to Consider: It's important to consider the root causes of an issue when dealing with student behavior. How can educators take the time to ask students about their behavior and

Students may not have all the answers at the time that we expect answers, but if you trust the process and assess what needs to be examined, they will come through for you with incredible alternative insights—things that we often wouldn't think of on our own. The partnership between students and educators is essential for reform, rejuvenation, or transformation.

support their students even after they mess up? How can teachers work against the temptation to label certain kids as troublemakers?

Voice Activator Reflections: Share a story with your students about a time when you messed up as a kid. What are some ways you can help them understand that making mistakes is part of life, but that mistakes are also opportunities for growth? Sometimes students don't realize that. Try talking to your students about how you learned from some of your own mistakes. When you share your own experiences and plotlines with your students, you can activate student voice in powerful ways.

COMMUNITY-SERVICE COMPETITION AND AWARDS GONE AWRY

To be useful, student voice must be open and honest. What might be perceived as just students complaining is actually important information being imparted from children to adults. To discern what young people are truly trying to say, adults have to step back and listen in a nonjudgmental way. It's only then that the power of student voice can come through and provide us with insights we had never before considered. We guarantee that you will learn new things and alternative perspectives. You just will!

Like the antibullying programs that have grown so popular across the nation, another initiative—community-service requirements for graduation—is also causing anxiety for some students. To get into the National Honor Society or similar organizations, students at high schools everywhere must meet a community-service requirement. Since 2005, scores of schools across the country are now making that same requirement a school-wide condition of graduation. Touted as a surefire way to prepare students for the workforce, it's now part of career-based learning principles that are supposed to get students ready for the real world. With honorable intentions of setting up such programs, indeed, are we maybe missing something about such a requirement?

Something interesting struck us when speaking to high school students in Newark, New Jersey, during a student assembly about the *Let Them Speak!* Project. In a few high schools, graduation-ceremony awards would be given to graduating seniors who had the most community-service hours documented in the counselor's office by the end of senior year. Twelfth grader, Elissa, offers an interesting look at how community service is treated by students and their parents at her school:

> Some of my friends go crazy about getting their community-service hours in. They want to get into a good college and know that getting the community-service award will look good on their transcript and résumé. So it becomes cutthroat. Some of my friends even get their parents to sign off on stuff they never did just so they can increase their service hours. I've seen kids log over 500, 600 hours so they will come out on top. There are three awards given: gold, silver, and bronze. I'd say 600 will get you the gold. So everyone strives to get there. It's kinda like a big joke among us. The amount of time kids spend on plotting how to get the most hours could probably be better spent doing something else. I do service, myself, yeah, but I don't turn into a nutcase about it. It's like a crazy competition that becomes obsessive. Lying, cheating, and all sorts of false documentation exist and the people who hand out the awards are clueless about what we kids are laughing about at the end of the day. It needs to be changed. The whole program needs to be revamped.
>
> **—Elissa, Grade 12**

What started out as a well-intentioned program by adults actually became a joke to the students. We aren't poking fun at this outcome or scolding schools that provide awards like this, but it is incredibly interesting that students were so bothered and annoyed by what really happened as a result of this adult-driven programming decision. Something as simple as providing awards in school became more complex than anyone ever expected. Maybe the educators and students wouldn't have known this at the beginning of setting up community-service programming and maybe student voice at the onset of setting up such programming would have never recognized any potential flaws. But, what we want to share with you about this example is that student voice came into play while such programming unfolded. Our point is: It is never too late to activate student voice at any stage of a process in order to improve anything that we do.

Examining Plotlines

Plotlines and outcomes don't always have to save a situation from the start. Activating student voice can come into play at any stage of the game. Think about programming that has operated at your school for a long time. Do you need to resuscitate it in some way? Find out new angles to an older problem? Figure out and assess how things are going right now? It is never too late to flip the switch on for accessing student voice. Adjustments can be made at any time!

The Student Voice Plotline: "Kids will sometimes find ways to win. They will sometimes find advantages of skewing something to better suit their own needs. I don't want to be wrapped up in this kind of thing and that's why I didn't participate as much as I could have in this program. I should get an award for doing the right thing and not cheating my way to the top."

What We Need to Consider: Could giving out awards for the most community service have the reverse effect on a student body? Should we ask students if they enjoy doing community service or what they're getting out of the experience? What if we asked students to provide input about other awards and recognitions that exist at our schools?

Voice Activator Reflections: Are there things you do in your classroom or school that seem positive but might really have a different effect on your students? Set aside time to assess anything at any stage of the process so students can tell you what they think about recognition, awards, competition, or anything that we've discussed in this chapter.

Chapter 5
Crushing the (Sometimes Invisible) Status Quo

If you're not upsetting anyone, you're not changing the status quo.

–Seth Godin

Since the first chapter of this book, we have been deliberately building a crescendo for supporting the underlying theme of our work: It is most import to build relationships with students to explore new ways to transform instruction, programming, and the functioning of our schools to better meet students' needs. In this chapter—a chapter devoted to crushing the status quo—we hit our climatic high note.

We believe that this entire book is about crushing the status quo. We must drill down even further to unveil what that means for classroom teachers, administrators, and students to actually reckon with what we believe is an *invisible* status quo. You probably know where this discussion is going. What's the most common response to challenging the status quo? We say we want to eradicate it, but sometimes we don't know what that really means. If you're an educator, you've definitely heard about getting rid of the status quo before and might have said it yourself a time or two:

But, we've always done it this way [or that way]!

Honestly, these words send shivers up our spines and make our stomachs turn. We dislike this type of mindset so much. When we reflected on our own reactions—to that lame response and the idea of doing things the same way—we wondered what students might think about our capabilities to teach and lead them while having their best interests in mind. Don't get us wrong: If something is working well, there is no need to change it. We know that and our students know that too. The problem isn't that things are okay being untouched. The problem is that we don't ask kids if we *should* touch an issue or not.

COULDN'T IT BE DONE DIFFERENTLY IF . . . ?

At a small rural school in New Salem, North Dakota, Jenny Schumaker, an eleventh-grade math teacher, realized that her math students were struggling when they had to take chemistry during their junior year. As juniors, they also prepared for the SATs, took as many electives as possible, and doubled up on coursework that gave them the best shot at the colleges they would be applying to in the fall of their senior year. Jenny regularly saw students walk down the hallway with long faces after getting out of chemistry class as they talked about how chemistry was killing them. It didn't seem to matter who the teacher was; it was simply a hard course for many juniors and even harder for those who didn't enjoy science. Between the lab time needed and the thick textbook everyone hated, chemistry quickly

Many schools across America participate in spelling bees. We are not mocking spelling proficiency pursuits, but why not hold contests on who can assemble an engine the quickest or put a computer together in record time? Why do we always do the same thing just because we've done it for years? An engine, computer, or anything else is just as important as spelling, and that should be celebrated too.

became one of the all-time most hated subjects in the school's history, even though taking chemistry during junior year was what *always* had been done since the dawn of time.

Even more disturbing was when students entered high school as ninth graders: they would hear about the horrors of junior year—with chemistry being the number one reason to loathe eleventh grade. This perception and problem consumed Jenny and she spent a great deal of time thinking about how to end the cycle of student fear that she had witnessed as a teacher for the previous seven years of her career.

One day, Jenny went to eat lunch in the junior/senior lounge just across the hall from the gymnasium where lots of boys shot hoops when they had a free period. She went in with a few simple questions designed to activate student voice and reckon with this chemistry conundrum. Here is what she asked her students:

1. What would help you to succeed in chemistry?
2. How can I, as your math teacher, help you in chemistry?
3. What solutions do you have for making your junior year a little more enjoyable?

The answers Jenny received were incredible, and she sent us her students' stories—some of which we decided to use in this book to illustrate how student voice can transform both the happiness and success of students—along with a school-wide academic program that needed a vitamin B-12 shot. Take a look at how this turning-point discussion unfolded:

Scott: Phew! That one is easy. Lose chemistry or the guy who decided that kids need to take it in school—let alone their junior year when we have so many pressures as it is, more so than in ninth or tenth grade. [Laughing.] No, seriously, well, why do we have to take chemistry in eleventh grade if at all? I mean, I want to become a news reporter. Chemistry isn't going to help me to become a news reporter. So as I think about your questions, maybe we should be allowed to take another science class instead of chemistry. Like maybe physics. I think I would like to take physics more, anyway, even if I don't like science.

Roman: Yeah, man. I'll second that. I know I'd rather skip chemistry altogether, but Mr. Frederick [the counselor] told me that every eleventh grader has to take chemistry. It is part of our science sequence that we need to graduate.

Scott: So why can't we replace chemistry with physics?

Dwight: Because physics is for seniors.

Scott: Who says?

Roman: I dunno. It's just the way it is, the way they always have done it. It's in the course handbook.

Scott: Well, that's a stupid rule. Why can't we change the rule and just take physics?

Jenny: Hold that thought! I'll be right back! [Leaves the gym.]

Inspired by her students' pushback, Jenny went to the school's principal and counselor with a few ideas. After some brainstorming, they came up with a two-fold plan that would give students the following options to making their junior year a bit more bearable:

Option 1: A new combined math/applications to science course would become a new course for any students who needed support. If staffing couldn't be increased at that moment, Jenny volunteered to teach an additional class each day to catch students up.

Option 2: Allow students to take advanced biology or physics instead of chemistry in their junior year in order to achieve their three-course sequence in science before they graduated.

Some pushback was created by the science teachers in the department who didn't want to give up their flexibility in just teaching seniors physics or creating combined courses that no one had approved. The board of education needed to approve such curriculum changes and such course content would need to be devised at least one year prior to any new changes. While the solution seemed simple, the process that adults created for setting up policies, seeking approval, or innovating new ideas trumped the timeliness of activating student voice and forging ahead with immediate versus delayed solutions.

The bad news is that changes at Jenny's school did not take place overnight. The good news is that Jenny worked diligently to create new course content for the following year that was sent to the board of education for approval, and a new math/applications science course started the following year. A few board members did vote against the idea, falling back on the argument of, "That's not how we've always done it! I took chemistry in eleventh grade, so why can't these kids do it?"

Educators who fight for creative solutions will always get resistance from colleagues who are fundamentally opposed to change or who truly believe the status quo is working well. But at Jenny's school, student voice was the catalyst that spurred the adults to take action. Student voice generated a realistic solution, fired up a teacher to make it happen, and then ultimately instituted a change that would help students for future years to come. The success rate of juniors who took physics was increased substantially, and no one really knew why. What they did know was students were no longer failing chemistry in their junior year, because the adults activated student voice and created program reform in order to stimulate student learning and customer satisfaction.

Examining the Plotlines

Our own systems can delay immediate action that is healthy for transforming student learning.

The Student Voice Plotline: "There is no good reason why I have to take chemistry in my junior year. My friends and I are all struggling. Why can't we take a different course? Can you look into this for me?"

What We Need to Consider: Do we, inadvertently, set up barriers that block forward thinking and throw sand on our students' natural thirst for progress?

Voice Activator Reflections: Does your classroom or school have long-standing systems that have always functioned in the same way? What are some rules or policies that you believe could be reasonably changed or improved? How can you work toward a creative solution to combat unproductive systems? How can you incorporate student voice into finding a solution to the barriers that block systemic change?

POLICIES, SCHMOLICIES

The most interesting thing about rules is that for every rule we create, there is always a really good reason to break it.

The chemistry conundrum at Jenny's school was a good example of what we like to call *policy exhaustion*. Policy exhaustion happens when systems create policies for a particular reason but then let them die in dusty manuals on crowded shelves. Rarely do school districts and many other organizations take the time to update or revisit policies for the sake of making *reformative* improvements instead of just only *revision* improvements (e.g., updating policy-effective dates).

We instead let policies sit idle for years or even decades until a major problem surfaces.

Policy exhaustion is common. The funny thing is that most policies are written to protect or keep something *safe*. It is when policies strangle, suffocate, or bind us to things that only end up micromanaging our daily routines that we shoot ourselves in the foot. Have you ever looked at a policy manual in your district? We would bet almost anything that your school or district policy manual is thicker than any concrete slab on your school property. Or, you have a digital policy folder that is rarely opened unless something negative happens in our schools, and we must "look up the policy to prove how right we are about something." Wouldn't it be interesting if we all started the school year backwards—reading policies with our students to find silly stuff that needs updating, deletion, or reformation? To remove the barriers and open up the floodgates of real growth, we cannot sit back and let policy construction determine our students' fate.

In general, school policies are created by adults but have the most impact on students, who, unfortunately, are rarely involved in the process of getting rid of wrong-headed policies. That's why we need to bring students into policy-construction discussions. The rules and requirements that we write about affect our students on a daily basis, so wouldn't *their* viewpoints be useful for us?

The following student voices, mined by Randy, superintendent of schools in a Missouri school district, remind us there are still plenty of policies in place that do nothing to protect student learning, but everything to prohibit real school transformations:

> Why are students suspended (out of school) for not coming to school or being late to school, according to our attendance policy?
>
> **—Jonah, Grade 9**

Why are students not allowed to eat or drink in the gymnasium? This is exactly the place where Gatorade and protein bars work their magic!

—Elizabeth, Grade 12

Why do I get busted for coming in to school with a cup of coffee, but get off the hook when my teacher sends me out to get coffee for her and a few teachers at the Dunkin' Donuts right next to our school?

—Cameron, Grade 12

If I get suspended from something I did wrong at the senior field trip, why am I not allowed to attend graduation? Why? Because graduation takes place within the five-day suspension that I received so I'm not allowed to be on school property or attend school events according to the discipline policy.

—Dana, Grade 12

Why do I have to get a physical from the school doctor and not my own doctor, according to the health/wellness policy in our district?

—Sammy, Grade 8

Why are kids allowed to stay in class when they have lice?

—Klara, Grade 5

Why was my mom's best friend not allowed to pick me up from school during an emergency just because her name wasn't on my emergency card? I know her really well. It's not like she was a stranger trying to kidnap me.

—Eloise, Grade 5

This sampling of problems and issues related to policies that we cling to not only demands how we should revisit those policies, it demands we should consider student voice. We have to always strive to solicit students' thoughts and opinions about the rules that directly impact virtually every part of their school day. In reality, most of these policy problems don't have quick solutions, but listening to students' narratives makes the issues come alive in a new way. Looking through the lens of student voice also helps us realize how many of our policies are really "schmolicies."

Examining the Plotlines

Artificial manuals or digital folders that contain thousands of school policy guidelines and rules are often untouched by us until something happens, and we need to reference a policy to cover our backs. The status quo relies on this very type of complacency.

The Student Voice Plotline: "I don't understand this rule. It seems silly to me, but you might have a good reason for such a policy. Do you? But if you don't have a good reason, can we revise it or throw it out? Can we look at it together? Policies impact me, you know. I'd love to give you some input on how we can make our school better."

What We Need to Consider: In what ways might we think about assembling a policy team to uncover the potential silliness that was created years ago and have students actively participate in policy construction or deletion?

Voice Activator Reflections: What is one example of a policy in your school that doesn't make a whole lot of sense or one that ostracizes students? Ask your students what they think about it, and record some of their responses. Consider asking your students to tell you about a policy that they think is strange and then work out some ways to revise it. What are some ways to make your classroom and school culture more accepting of such an innovation after policy analysis?

Loopholes are the product of isolation, conformity, and limitations.

COMMUNAL CHEATING

In the story below, you will find a narrative written by a student named Walter that mentions the 1992 movie *School Ties* and the powerful series of scenes about cheating and adhering to the school's honor code. You can check it out here: youtu.be/fSCd-DmtiBA.

Competitiveness in schools can often strangle students. When we cultivate unhealthy competition, it breeds a cutthroat world that instigates students to come up with new annual honor code signatures to conform to the deity of a test. It doesn't encourage or cultivate positive communal cheating which we contend has a place in schools and in student learning frameworks. We go along with traditional testing methods, individually testing students with desks situated in rows, as a routine practice in our classrooms. It emphasizes the need to be right rather than cultivating the power of collaborative learning for the sake of becoming a lifelong learner. State standardized testing typically occurs once each year as a state mandate, but we don't have to standardize our students as a routine practice in our classrooms.

Below, Walter, a twelfth grader, mentions theorist and Russian scholar, Lev Vygotsky, and how Vygotsky's scholarly friends would meet in the public squares of Moscow to form think tanks, collaborate, and learn within communal constructs. Sure, tests and private, individualized measurements of student learning have existed for years and are still a reality today. But maybe it doesn't always have to be that way.

In a private Catholic school just outside of Boston, Massachusetts, Headmaster Colden Jones was adamant about having each and every student sign a code of honor at the summer orientation that decreed that no student would cheat on any coursework or any assessments given to them over the course of the entire school year. When students returned to school the following year, they had to update and recertify this code of honor with a new, fresh signature.

Cheating was frowned upon and was not only supported as a major creed of the school, it was also a form of incredible policy violation if any student was caught cheating. While cheating was considered an egregious act where students would be permanently expelled from school, a few students thought differently about the idea of cheating. Take a look at what some students said about "cheating" when their teacher, Kevin Tompkins, asked them these questions:

1. What is cheating?
2. When is cheating not OK?
3. When is cheating not really cheating?

Walter's voice made such an impact on Kevin and on us that we wanted to share his thoughts within this chapter:

> I remember learning how Russian scholars would hold communal discussions in the center square of their cities, great thinkers like Vygotsky, thinkers who focused on dualism and the power that others have over total social learning. Yet in school, we are so individualized. Desks in rows, maybe not every day, but most certainly during testing time. Yet when I think about testing in general, I'm unclear as to why testing still pervades our schools today. I thought we'd come a long way from locking up tests to

signing pledges or codes of honor like in the movie *School Ties* that I saw on television a while back. It kinda made me think about my school and how competitiveness is linked to testing, which is linked to the notion of what cheating is really about. But if we embark on a new era of education, where communal learning is not considered cheating, where testing is no longer individualized, where Vygotsky wouldn't roll in his grave, I tend to think schools are just as smug as they used to be in this way. To cheat or not to cheat makes me wonder if to learn or not to learn—with others—is the real question.

—Walter, Grade 12

This narrative speaks to us on so many levels. First, Walter is brilliant. He gets it! His grasp of vocabulary is awesome and commendable, on the one hand, and on the other hand, his voice, now formally documented for you in this book, demonstrates the knowledge that students can bring to the table in almost any topical area; in fact, we are wondering if we should submit Walter's narrative voice to some sort of research journal for further follow-up! If we could track him down today, we would certainly love for him to read this book and advocate alongside us about the power of student voice.

Examining the Plotlines

When we label and pigeonhole a practice as "wrong," it prevents us from thinking about how to move forward with new transformations to our classrooms and schools.

The Student Voice Plotline: "I'm not a cheater. I'm actually trying to learn. If what you want to do is test me on memorizing facts—dates, places, people, and events—why do I have to memorize anything when I have access to information at lightning speed on my smartphone? Why are calculators not allowed? Why do I have to pretend that I cannot get information right at my fingertips? Our world has changed. We don't need to use paper and pencil on something we can get on our own, digitally. We aren't cheaters. We are consumers of knowledge and information."

What We Need to Consider: Are there times when traditional "no-no's" should no longer apply to the schools of today? When is it okay to re-evaluate traditional norms and become more flexible when specific circumstances might push against old, absolute policies or norms?

Voice Activator Reflections: Can you think of instances where cheating really isn't cheating? Can you also think of other communal activities where learning should be stressed versus rote memory or testing activities? Can you ask your students to define cheating and identify what it is and isn't? Can you work with your school on trying to figure out what cheating really is and what we've historically classified as cheating versus communal learning? What are some ways your school evaluates how the Internet is accessed, how smartphones should be used, and how learning is now more communal than it used to be? Do you ban calculators and smartphones that HAVE calculators?

Inclusion isn't about high-needs students simply being in the same classrooms as any other student. It is about intentionally planning for the individual success of all students.

SPECIAL EDUCATION AND IEP ACCOMMODATIONS

It was fourth period and close to the end of the day, and Trent, a sixth-grade, special-education inclusion student, just lost it. The teacher had facilitated a lesson on determining the area of trapezoids by using a composition of rectangles and triangles to solve the problems. Mrs. Nellie had modeled the steps and even projected a simulation from "Illustrative Mathematics" and had small groups practice a couple problems using manipulatives. She was gradually releasing them to work independently and handed out the worksheet so everyone could start on the assignment.

Although Trent's IEP called for chunking the assignment into smaller pieces, that day Mrs. Nellie was running late and forgot. Some days she remembered and altered the assignment ahead of time, and other times, she ran off the assignment last minute and handed Trent the same work as everyone else. On this particular day, Trent's lack of accommodations triggered his anxiety. After Mrs. Nellie walked by and placed the assignment on his desk, he just sat there with his head down. After she noticed he still wasn't working, she walked by and tapped her nails on his desk and told him to get to work. He still didn't lift a finger. Mrs. Nellie gave him two choices: He could either go to the back table and do the worksheet, or he could sit there and do the worksheet, but doing nothing was not an option. Trent got angry, stood up, and began tipping over a few desks. Mrs. Nellie immediately buzzed the front office to get help dealing with Trent's dangerous behavior. The assistant principal came down and escorted Trent to the cool-down room and he left willingly. When he was calm, she had him walk the halls with her and go to the cafeteria to get lunch and eat with a different grade level.

During lunch, the assistant principal had a casual conversation with Trent and asked him the following questions:

1. What emotions were you feeling this morning when tipping the desks over?
2. What caused you to feel that way?
3. What can we do to help you be more successful in Mrs. Nellie's class?

Here's what Trent had to say:

> I don't know why my palms turned sweaty, my heart started racing, and I just blanked out for a minute. Every step closer my teacher got to my desk, I got more scared and mad. The assignment was too hard I didn't get it. I understood parts, but about halfway through the lesson, I just spaced out. Usually Mrs. Nellie walks to the corner of her desk to get my assignment that is different than the other kids. I just do one part at a time, but today she walked by and handed out the same long assignment in the tiniest print. I mean the directions alone looked smaller than the print in the dictionary. I just freaked out. I knew I couldn't do it and I knew she wasn't prepared to help me. I could tell she just wanted me to sit down and do it even though I couldn't. She just wanted to go back to her desk and check her cell phone like she always does. My mom is always calling the school and complaining about the work. She doesn't think that I can hear her but I have overheard her saying things like, "It's the law," and "You have to be consistent or he won't be successful." I know the only reason my teacher even chunks my work or allows me to use a computer is because of my mom. My teacher doesn't even really want to do any extra work to help me. She just wants me to be like all the other kids and

I'm not. The only thing that could help me in her class is to replace her with a teacher that understands that I don't want to panic or get angry. Someone that really wants to help me learn rather than get on her cell phone. She just puts up with me; she doesn't really care at all. To her, I'm just a problem, not a person.

—Trent, Grade 6

Here, Trent opened up because he was allowed to. How often do we enable students to tell us what they're thinking, or why they acted a certain way? Sometimes simply giving students the freedom to speak candidly provides the skeleton key to all the doors that need to be unlocked.

Examining the Plotlines

Everything happens for a reason and students can tell us exactly what is happening with them. Student voice can highlight times of need. Student voice does not exist to only solve problems or provide restorative input.

The Student Voice Plotline: "If you really want to know the truth, I don't even like myself. I hate when I shut down every time something seems hard. I just want teachers to understand me and that I can't control the way I feel. I want to learn, but it is twice as scary to me. I can tell when an adult is doing something out of compliance or because they care. I'm not stupid. I am different from the other kids and require much more attention and strategies. Am I worth the extra work? Please . . . can you help me?"

What We Need to Consider: How can you meet the individual needs of your special-education inclusion students to ensure that their basic needs of safety, security, and love are being met? What do you still need to learn about neuroscience and why kids do what they do? How can you forge a relationship with the most difficult students in class? What instructional strategies do you still need to learn that may be helpful to special-education students? What backlash might you have to face for not effectively implementing a child's Individual Education Plan? Can you ask your students what they need, why they need it, and how you can help?

Voice Activator Reflections: Do you have a toolbox of strategies that will help you connect with students with disabilities, cognitive learning deficits, or poor regulation of emotions? What's inside this toolbox and have you asked your students about the tools they need? How does consistency impact your students? What happens when you are inconsistent? Do your special-education students know you care? How do you give them opportunities to drive their learning and growth? How are you giving them the freedom to tell you what they need?

FIDGET SPINNERS

Out of nowhere, these whizzing "distractions" invaded nearly every classroom like hostile aliens from outer space. And they kept multiplying and morphing into every color, size, and shape imaginable. It was an overnight sensation. We spoke with Mr. Knight, a third-grade math teacher in Chicago, Illinois, who took this invasion personally and stepped up as Commander in Chief of Fidget-Spinner Eradication. In the teacher workroom, you could hear him say things like, "I just don't get it. Why are these kids obsessed with these spinners? What is the fascination with this gimmick? It's making a joke of our profession. We are here to learn, not play." Students were only allowed to get them out at recess, lunch, or snack time in Mr. Knight's class.

Mr. Knight's principal, Mrs. Holland, was fascinated by this new trend and showed up at recess with her very own fidget spinners to see what these third-grade students had to say. Any principal with a fidget spinner has got to be cool, so who wouldn't want to talk to her? Take a look at what one student had to say about all of this:

> I don't get why we can't have them out in class. I mean, it keeps me from tearing up my worksheets into tiny little bits of paper when I have to listen to Mr. Knight talk about the history of Illinois. I tear up the little bits of paper inside my desk because it helps me listen. He doesn't see me because my hands are inside my desk, but it helps me to not be so bored when I have to sit for so long. At church, I use my fidget spinner and I can sit through the whole sermon without getting into trouble once and I even remembered what it was about.
>
> **—Frank, Grade 3**

> Fidget spinners are just cool. I want to be accepted by the kids in my class, so I have one. I don't want to be the nerd or a target for jokes. My friends all have them. I begged my mom for one and when I brought home an A+, a one hundred percent on my math test, she ordered one for me off Amazon. I picked the pink one with silver stars. It was quite cool, I might add. I don't use it all the time, but I have it on my desk so that I am not made fun of in class.
>
> **—Bridgette, Grade 3**

> My dad is a gifted teacher at another school and his students get to actually use them to do math. They did this entire unit on fidget spinners and he said it was the most learning he had ever seen in his kids. So I don't understand that if their school gets to use them to learn, why we can't. My dad even talked about how many of his teacher

friends on Twitter were sharing cool fidget-spinner activities. He showed me some of the video clips and pictures. It looked so cool. He did a couple of the lessons with me at home and it was fun. I wish we could do fun lessons like that at school rather than read our boring textbooks and do worksheets all day long.

—Daniel, Grade 3

These narratives spoke volumes to Mrs. Holland. It was clear that there were many relevant reasons why her students wanted to use fidget spinners, although Mr. Knight saw it only as a gimmicky distraction. Because it was a controversial school-wide issue, and Mr. Knight wasn't the only teacher who felt that way, Mrs. Holland decided to share the student narratives with teachers during a faculty meeting. She opened the discussion by asking teachers their opinions about how the school should handle fidget-spinner *offenses*— if students should be allowed to use them during school hours or in different spaces of the school, such as the hallways and library. Several teachers said that they didn't care if students used them, but others said that they found it too distracting. Some teachers found them annoying because when one went missing, a student would go ballistic, crying and searching for it. In some cases, if the spinner broke, the entire day was shot. Many teachers felt like banning them altogether would just be easier.

After Mrs. Holland flushed out the students' frustrations, she simply asked, "Have you asked your students what they think?" You could have heard a pin drop as most of the teachers squirmed in their seats. She went on to read the student narratives, then read aloud from a blog written by a teacher who shared lesson plans, classroom pictures, and hyperlinks to videos of how to incorporate fidget spinners into daily learning. In one lesson, students used their spinners as timers, racing and filling in a times-table grid. Next, they graphed their fidget-spinner data and discussed the variables of human error and individual spinner design. Those lessons had one hundred percent student engagement.

During the faculty meeting, Jane Evans, the school counselor, chimed in and talked about the number of students in the building who had trouble self-regulating emotions and sensory needs and quoted an article that promoted the use of the fidget spinners as a tool to support these regulation needs. The outcome of the meeting was an agreement to embrace the fidget spinner trend and meet with their students during advisory periods to develop a few classroom norms on having the spinners in class as well as brainstorm all the ways that they could use them as part of their learning. They were tasked with reporting back the following week with at least one lesson that integrated these magical whirly birds.

We didn't share this scenario to try and convince you to use fidget spinners, but rather to capture the relevant concept that Denis Sheeran shares with us in his book *Instant Relevance*. Trends and fads provide us with opportunities to capitalize on them when they infiltrate your school. Why do we fight the issues that we think are small and watch them escalate into student unhappiness?

The secret to motivating students is to find out what is working in their ecosystem and breathe life into any particular trend of the classroom ecosystem.

Examining the Plotlines

Sometimes, we battle things that can actually assist us with making connections with kids. While the world is changing each day, we owe our students fresh perspectives on innovative education, not traditionally sustained educational systems.

The Student Voice Plotline: "I'm really not being disrespectful and I really can hear you whether I have a fidget spinner in my hand or not. I know the information is important for me to learn, but when I have to sit there for so long, I have to do something with my hands so I don't get bored. If we can't use fidget spinners, could we do something different so we don't have to just sit there?"

What We Need to Consider: What do you need to know about student motivation and how it links to student performance and achievement? How can you involve your classroom as a community when new trends do arise? How will you determine if it is appropriate to incorporate, and how will students be involved with the decision-making process?

Voice Activator Reflections: How important is it to keep up with the fads and trends that students embrace which don't appear to be school related? How can you teach academic content standards and still incorporate what's cool in student ecosystems? How can you rethink what you think are small, meaningless topics into big issues that your students want to discuss or address? Their worlds are bigger than we think, so in what ways can we pick apart anything that could motivate them to be and do their very best?

Chapter 6
Celebrating Student Diversity and Individuality

**To be yourself in a world that is constantly
trying to make you into something else
is the greatest accomplishment.**

–Ralph Waldo Emerson

The *Let Them Speak!* Project discovered student voices that not only celebrated diversity and individuality in students' schools, but it also advocated for their peers and defended their honor. Student voices remind their school communities that *all* students—even those who are drastically different from the mainstream—deserve to be treated with dignity and respect. To gather these narratives, we stuck to what worked for us and, once again, we talked to kids on their turfs—whether they were students who identified as LGBTQ or those have been labeled by others as "goth," "nerds," "geeks," or "techies." We met them where they like to hang out, chill out, or have fun, and we were honored to receive students' narrativized stories from all walks of life that can help transform schools everywhere.

LGBTQ STUDENT VOICES

We want to start with a powerful and emotional issue—one that garnered much media attention in the winter of 2017 when the Trump administration withdrew guidance on the issue of facility choice for LGBTQ students regarding lavatory and locker-room access. Many schools across the nation wanted to protect the rights of LGBTQ students, while other schools acted more punitively towards these students.

While this issue is certainly controversial in nature, we wanted to simply highlight the voices of students who were able to transcend this discussion within their own schools—demonstrating how students can come up with alternate solutions for even the most controversial matters.

Brenda Jarenka, a high school principal in Virginia, shared some of her students' voices with us when she discovered that her students were seeking different outcomes outside of the position that Gavin Grimm, a transgender student who sued his school board in the same region after he was denied access to the boys' bathroom at his school.[1] For the following reasons, student voice contributed to settling a controversial issue well beyond what any adult decided to do on their own if they were to make the decision in a vacuum regarding what students should feel comfortable doing in school. Take a look at these narratives:

---

1   Moira Balingit, "Why Laverne Cox Told You to Google 'Gavin Grimm,'" *The Washington Post*, February 12, 2017, washingtonpost.com/news/education/wp/2017/02/12/why-laverne-cox-told-you-to-google-gavin-grimm/?tid=a_inl&utm_term=.d5d6ae01986f.

While I have rights and should be able to enter into the lavatory that I identify with the most, I also feel like I need to protect myself and rethink what I can do as a student in a school who should also feel safe and comfortable.

—Jeanne, Grade 10

My position is that I would like to have access to the nurse's office lavatory where there is one toilet inside a locked door that can be used by male, female, or any LGBTQ student.

—Stewart, Grade 11

I just want to feel normal, like everyone else when dealing with normal, everyday issues. Not sure why going to the bathroom is causing such a ruckus at our school, but if you ask me—and I know many of my friends who are LGBTQ also agree and even told me at one of our meetings—I opt for making the one-toilet lavatories with their own locks that both male and female staff members use to be a student-used lavatory, as well. That way, it gives us privacy and doesn't make me feel uncomfortable. We see these lavatories wherever we go now, anyway. Restaurants have them, hospitals have them, and some arenas and movie theaters have them too.

—Tasha, Grade 12

Principal Brenda Jarenka sought student voice as a driving force in the decisions she would make at her school, and she shared these student narratives with her faculty. Because of her advocacy and leadership style, this LGBTQ bathroom issue became a nonissue for Brenda's school, while other schools across the nation experienced challenges that were unsettled. Brenda's school did not have parent complaints or referrals in the office for accusations. It wasn't anything that administration needed to address, because it wasn't a point of conflict, unlike one particular school in a neighboring county that had to deal with parent and community backlash all over social media about their LGBTQ bathrooms. It was so bad that it caused a divide of opposing forces, which ended up targeting students off campus. Let's just say it was all over the news.

Students speak the truth, they reason, and they share with us their deepest feelings when we recognize that their words matter. They can help shift a community, protect a community, and even save a community. What one labels as a human-rights issue must also be balanced against what makes students feel comfortable and safe. At Brenda Jarenka's school, student comfort and safety was easily activated through student voices because she wondered what her students would say, and when they told her what they thought, it all made sense.

Examining the Plotlines

Students can open our eyes to perspectives that might be clouded by the degree of controversy. Don't be afraid to ask our, students what they think about issues that we might first shy away from presenting to them.

The Student Voice Plotline: "We have a solution that you might not have thought of. We don't want to create animosity in our school. We have rights, yes, but we also want to minimize bullying or opposition by not acting hastily. When you ask us for an opinion, we like sharing our thoughts. We like working together with the adults who are entrusted to care for us and protect us."

What We Need to Consider: Are there times when controversial topics can be presented to our students so they can assist us with finding solutions? In what ways can we look at all of the issues that might plague a school or school district and activate student voice outlets to provide us with insights we might never think of ourselves?

Voice Activator Reflections: Can you think of any controversial issues that took place in your classroom, school, or district over the past few months or years and ask your students what they think about those issues? Can we activate student voice in the decision-making process for tackling any type of controversial issue?

STUDENTS OF POVERTY

Do we know what low socio-economic status (SES) students really think about poverty? We know the impact poverty has on our system, as a whole, and understand Maslow's hierarchy of needs and how it affects learning. But have you ever wondered what students think and how they *feel* about living in poverty? How can our knowledge of their perceptions assist our instruction and leadership?

Poverty is like punishment for a crime you didn't commit.

—Eli Khamarov

A BOTTOMLESS CUP OF DIGNITY

Tonia, an eleventh grader from Tennessee, blew us away when she opened up to us about living in poverty. Look at what she has to say about her current life situation:

> I know I am poor. I mean, you can just look at my address and know that. And yeah, life is hard. It sucks to be poor. But just because I am poor doesn't mean I am dumb

or people should feel sorry for me. That's why I love Mrs. Spiegl. She gets me. In the past, my other teachers would give me supplies even if I didn't need them, and after I shared my story, they would feel sorry for me and send extra food home with me. Sometimes teachers would go out of their way to buy me extra fun and cute supplies, which was nice, but then the other kids would just pick on me and tell me it was just because I was poor. I didn't like how it made me feel because it pointed out the fact that I was poor even more, and I felt like I owed the teacher something. But not Mrs. Spiegl. I know she knows I am poor, but she also knows that I am smart and she knows what I'm good at.

One time, in our science block, my teacher noticed how I had organized all the materials at the back counter. She didn't ask me to, I was just done early and I noticed it was a wreck and organized her supplies and papers. Boy, did she notice! She asked me later if she could hire me to organize her supplies at the end of the day, each day. So I stopped by after the final bell and helped organize her stuff again. While she was at her desk grading, we just talked. She asked me why I was such a good student. She asked me what I needed. I told her I just wanted my dignity. I shared my sucky life story, but she didn't start giving me handouts or freebies. Instead, she asked me to dream big and write down what I wanted in life. I told her I wanted to be able to make other people happy, to be able to support myself so other people wouldn't look at me with eyes of sorrow and pity. She began writing down words on a piece of paper: "organized, resilient, deep, purposeful, hopeful, smart, thoughtful, giving." And she looked up at me and said, "These are the things that many of my students may never learn. You already have every attribute necessary to not only be successful, but successful enough to help others."

She made a deal with me that day that if I came in and organized her supplies throughout the week, in return she would let me earn any supplies or things I needed, and that she would always be there to listen. Mrs. Spiegl gave me my dignity back. She believed in me, held me to a high expectation, and didn't treat me different. I was never a target in her class because I earned everything that I got.

—Tonia, Grade 11

Over time, this mentorship flourished. Knowing one of Tonia's goals was to someday help others, Mrs. Spiegl asked Tonia if she knew anyone else who might want after-school jobs helping other teachers. Without any hesitation, Tonia said she had three others in mind who also lived in her apartment complex who literally didn't have a nickel to their names.

The next day, Tonia showed up with all three friends just as she said, and they went and worked in several of the teachers' classrooms doing various jobs from cleaning out the fish tank to labeling envelopes to cleaning off the desks. This became a weekly ritual, and the students really stepped up and willingly supported their school.

One day, Mrs. Spiegl talked to us about setting up these *internships* and said that her students were like interns because they were learning more about life and service behind the scenes. The students then started calling themselves "interns," and before you know it, that's what they were known for.

After school, Mrs. Spiegl's students got even more carried away and said they needed T-shirts so everyone would know they were interns. Mrs. Spiegl went to the principal and PTA and had T-shirts printed up for this group of juniors. No longer were they known for being poor. They were known for being school interns and school leaders.

No matter what socioeconomic status our students come from, they want to hold on to their dignity. Our students, who live in poverty, have something to tell us. Are we listening? Teacher perceptions changed regarding the roles that students held in this example, and in spite of socioeconomic differences, respect for those working as interns leveled the playing field, bringing about interpersonal respect among the entire school.

Examining the Plotlines

Standing out is a choice, and when choice is involved, classifications and labeling students can fade away. No longer do we want students to stand out like sore thumbs, rather, think of creative ways for respecting diversity in your classroom and school.

The Student Voice Plotline: "I really don't want to stand out. When I receive something for free, I have guilt that I owe you something back. If I earn something, then I feel like it's OK. If you just give it to me like I'm a charity case, I feel bad about myself. Can you help me become successful on my own so I can earn something and feel like it is mine? Do you notice anything about me other than my address from the other side of the tracks?"

What We Need to Consider: What do you need to learn about your students to ensure that your environment is caring and safe at all times? In what ways can you provide your students opportunities without them feeling like charity cases? How can you involve children of poverty in supporting others in need?

Voice Activator Reflections: How can you positively lead students from low SES backgrounds?

Rainbows are meant to be colorful, or else they wouldn't be rainbows.

RACISM IN SCHOOLS

As much as we want to believe segregation, racism, and hatred have been eradicated, the sad truth is they still exist within the walls of our schools. Educators are not overtly racist, nor do they intentionally segregate students or punish students for the color of their skin. But unless we are consciously in pursuit of equity, racism could still inadvertently exist. It still happens. It does. We affirmed this suspicion while visiting a preschool room in California. We hung out at the dress-up activity station in one particular classroom and asked, "Is there anything that we could change here?" Here's what several students had to say:

THE CLASS HELPER

I like dress-up, but I always want to be the office guy or the policeman, but the kids with white skin always take it first, so I always end up being the delivery guy or the dad.

—Trey, Pre-K

We should fix time-out. I think it is mostly for the brown kids. I see white kids be naughty and they don't have to leave. But me and my brown friends go to time-out a lot.

—Tatiana, Pre-K

I want my friend Sasha to be picked for class helper. She never gets picked. Is it because her skin is brown? The brown kids are not the helpers, at least not the ones chosen first.

—Rhianna, Pre-K

The Safe Schools Coalition[2] shares research on racism among young children. By the age of three, children notice physical differences:

> Learning about white superiority and black inferiority comes from informal lessons learned as whites grow up and mature, as children at home and school and as adults socializing with relatives and friends. However, a recent study of young white children in a preschool setting found that even three- to four-year-olds interact with children of other racial groups using clear and often sophisticated understandings of racist ideas and epithets.[3]

After collecting these narratives, we shared them with Anna White, the preschool teacher, and she decided to be more observant of her interactions as well as the students. The next time the kids were at centers, she specifically watched the dress-up station. And sure enough, there was evidence of superiority and inferiority taking place in her classroom even on her watch. She also went back to her records to discover that she was inadvertently supporting racist groupings.

The first quarter of school was already over, and the only students who had been chosen as helpers were white students. Anna knew she wasn't a racist. She truly loved all the students in her school, but discovering the inequity in her classroom led to some deep reflections after listening to her students. She incorporated more social stories about being a good friend and showing kindness, and she was intentional about equally calling on every ethnicity rather than who she noticed was behaving and should be rewarded as a result. Anna did

2   Theresa V. Lee, "Racism and Young Children: What Does the Research Say?", *Safe School Coalition*, 2008, safeschoolscoalition.org/Racism&YoungChildren-byTheresaLee.pdf.

3   Joe R. Feagin, *Racist America: Roots, Current Realities, and Future Reparations*. (New York: Routledge, 2014) 130-131.

not want to further solidify the inequity that already resides within her community.

Examining the Plotlines

Student voice activation should be blameless. We shouldn't beat ourselves up over realities unless we choose to turn our backs on reality and not address our new findings.

The Student Voice Plotline: "I am not inferior to anyone else. Can my peers learn about me—the true me? I like school best when we focus on helping each other. I believe we can all do important things, no matter where we come from or what we look like."

What We Need to Consider: Have we considered how superiority and inferiority still exist within our schools? What can we do about it? What can we ask students about their experiences with these two concepts? Can we explicitly challenge superiority constructs within our schools by just asking our students to confront these issues instead of not wanting to touch these powerful issues with a ten-foot pole?

Voice Activator Reflections: In what ways will you push boundaries and intentionally promote social justice in your day-to-day interactions with students? What kinds of questions can you ask your students to help them know you care about their greater good, their heritages, and their unique life experiences? How can you make it clear to your students that you aren't scared to touch the difficult issues to bring students together? Consider everything you do with students during the average school day, and reflect on how you can be more equitable and inclusive.

SECOND-LANGUAGE LEARNERS

As a border state to Mexico, Arizona is home to many English as a Second Language (ESL) students. The state mandates English Language Proficiency (ELP) standards and a four-hour block dedicated to learning Structured English Immersion (SEI). Teachers are required to teach listening, speaking, reading, writing, and language within a four-hour block, according to the Office of English Language Acquisition Services (OELAS). Among this group are many refugees who have recently arrived from Middle Eastern countries.

CELERY FOR ALL

Because language was such a barrier, we chose to speak with second-grade students who were successful at learning English, had been in an ESL program since kindergarten, and were close to exiting the program. We weren't able to work through translators; that is why we chose to speak with this small group of students. We asked a few girls who were in the library waiting for their teacher, "What is something you wish we could do better?" We kept it simple and wide open for any topic to be presented to us. Look at what these second graders said to us:

> In the hall, I see posters for science. Other kids do a lot of science with real stuff. We don't get to do the fun stuff with science in class. We only learn English and math. I want to learn science too. Even though I don't know good English, I can still see with my eyes and try to do it.
>
> **—Josie, Grade 2**

Yeah, me too. I had to bring a note to one of the other teachers and when I was in Mrs. Jones' class, I saw celery in colored water turning all sorts of colors. They even got to do a song and dance about plants. It looked like more fun. than we were having in our class.

—Juanita, Grade 2

I like to play with magnets and measure stuff. It's more fun than talking in English sentences and writing words over and over. Science looks fun.

—Rita, Grade 2

We certainly weren't going to make the girls write out their plotlines, so we quickly transcribed what they said to us in order to share this information with their teachers. These girls desperately wanted to learn science. How incredible is that? At the same time, their teachers were clearly striving to comply with the law.

Because compliance with laws and regulations is necessary, we knew we needed to turn this into a win-win situation. During a K–2 meeting, we shared the results of our meeting with the girls and read their narratives out loud. The outcome of the meeting was profound! The teachers started talking about the domains they were required to teach—reading, writing, speaking, listening, and language—and it was like a 1,000-megawatt lightbulb had been flipped on. Nearly in unison, they began saying that all of these domains are part of learning and teaching science. They began to realize it was just a matter of how to integrate science into the ESL four-hour block so students could learn English development through the practice of science. In the weeks to come, you couldn't have imagined how happy our second-grade friends were when exploring all kinds of science concepts labs, and experiments.

Examining the Plotlines

Requirements and mandates sometimes cloud our vision of providing exciting learning opportunities for all students.

The Student Voice Plotline: "Why can't I do the things that the other kids get to do in class? I like science too, and it looks fun. I like to pretend I'm doing science, even if I can't do it for real. Can we please do fun activities instead of just reading a book over and over again? I already feel different, and now I'm in a class where I feel even more different because I can't do the same fun things that the other kids get to do."

What We Need to Consider: Relationships and backgrounds matter even more with students where English is their second language. Often this comes with cultural differences, schema that may prevent understanding, and unwritten expectations. What can you do to better understand the perspective of each student culturally, ethnically, and as a second-language learner?

Voice Activator Reflections: In a profession with so many mandates and laws, are we doing what is best for kids? Are there times we can integrate subject areas to leverage best practices? What should we consider when teaching second-language learners? Are we forgetting to do something that will ignite student learning because we are looking at other pathways for achievement gains?

OPEN-TOED SHOES

Moving from intense stories about racism, diversity, students with disabilities, and English acquisition, we want to provide a quick snapshot about individuality by presenting an issue that might not seem important, at first, but truly is because of the negative impact that it has had on student motivation. Whether or not students should wear school uniforms is an age-old debate that has many pros and cons. While some high school dress-code policies are broad in language and more open to interpretation, others are more intricately detailed and enforced. Notice how Isaiah Sterling, the eleventh grader from Missouri whom we mentioned earlier in this book, shared his thoughts about his own high school dress code:

> At my high school, students have to follow a specific dress code. The code bans open-toed shoes, ripped jeans, V-neck tees, and pants that aren't navy, grey, or black. Since the code was enforced across the district, students have not stopped talking amongst themselves. As a student leader, I noticed that all this talk was distracting us from focusing on our academics. Not only academic time, but school culture. Our school culture has decreased (negatively) significantly. The code takes out of academic time because teachers are required to send kids to the office when they are not in compliance with the dress code. Sometimes educators will have to send four or five kids to the office during class time! With educators constantly cracking down on the dress code, students started to roll up in a ball and not speak out. Not once were we asked how we feel about the code. I am realizing that there is no system of trust. Without trust, we have nothing! My main message out of this entire situation is that educators should just ask us and listen to us! Students and parents have started to rebel against the code. Educators must ask why dress code is so important. They did just that, and now myself and other students are planning to meet with administrators monthly to work on ways we can improve school culture concerning the dress code so that less academic time isn't taking us away from what is really important in school.

> **—Isaiah, Grade 11**

While some of the other narratives had some type of resolution in some shape or form that ended positively, this issue is still an ongoing debate that is impacting the culture, climate, and the academics of students at Isaiah's school. We invite the school leaders there, or anywhere else that deals with dress-code plotlines, to consider analyzing these plotlines that will build better adult and student relationships.

Examining the Plotline

How do we come to a point where we make decisions based on what we think we know is best for students?

The Student Voice Plotline: "Let's get real. This is a game of power and control. Who is really winning in the end? Yes, there will always be a few kids who don't make responsible choices with the dress code, no matter the rules, but most of us will. Do you have good reasons for these rules? If our parents even agree with us, why can't you? Will our feet become severed because of open-toed shoes?"

What We Need to Consider: We must ask ourselves, "Is this a battle that really needs fighting?" Is what we are doing an issue of power and control, or is it within our control to uncover policy mandates and reasons? When we prohibit something for the sake of prohibiting, it only causes more resentment, severs relationships, and eliminates the possibility of ultimate success.

Voice Activator Reflections: In what ways can you look at your own reasons for rules in your classroom or school and rethink how they're affecting students? What are some ways you could have better outcomes than you already have now?

The spirit of student voice can also be a saving grace for teachers and school leaders across the nation. Student voice does not always need to solve problems or present alternative viewpoints. Student voice can heal, motivate, encourage, and even thank those who work hard each day to provide incredible experiences for children.

Chapter 7
Stories about Thanks, Gratitude, and Improvement

You must not lose faith in humanity. Humanity is like an ocean; if a few drops of the ocean are dirty, the ocean does not become dirty.

—Mahatma Gandhi

TO OUR TEACHERS WITH LOVE

This final chapter is about you, the educators and leaders who allow our students to ask some pointed questions about their customer service experiences in school. It is about getting human feedback by being direct and honest. It is about being vulnerable. It is about becoming better and knowing that we must be motivated to show up and excel each day. It is about incorporating a novel respect for student voice by injecting it into our professional creed and seeking ways to improve our craft through the mouths of our students. It is about taking action regardless of how high our work piles up. It is about relationships. Always.

Let Them Speak!

This chapter isn't for the faint of heart. It presents a discussion platform that we can have with our students without getting riled up about what they might say; in fact, this is one of our most memorable chapters ever written in any of our other books and we wanted to end with it because it balances the power of student voice with the happiness that a guttural transformation can bring to your school and even your *lives*. Where some of this book might call on you to wrestle with issues because it steps on toes, this chapter is different. We worked hard to design this book and report to you that listening to student voice matters in virtually every aspect of what we do in education. Student perception should help us to improve the way we do business. Sharing truths shouldn't hurt our feelings; it should celebrate and bring honor to the great work that we do each day.

So, what really stops us from asking students what they think about us? We are not saying we want them to comment on our hair color, whether or not we wear eyeglasses, or highlight stuff about our personal lives (e.g., whether we are married with three children or not). We want their insights about our teaching, our leadership of students, and the uniqueness of our craft. Their thoughts just might ignite a spark within us and cultivate a new love for the greatest profession on earth. We're only human, and even if there are a few dirty spots of reflection, it's worth every minute of turf-talking, voice-activating, and student-driven reflection opportunities for all of us.

SAGE ON THE STAGE

Jonathan Creswell, an eighth-grade teacher in Maryland, wanted to get some feedback from his students about his teaching practices. He went out on the field during a free period on a really hot spring day and asked two of his students, Jennifer and Roger, what they thought about him—his teaching, not anything personal, per se. Here is what he asked them to consider:

1. What are some things that you like that I do in class?
2. What do you like about me as a teacher and what don't you like about me as a teacher or wish that I did differently?

The second question is tougher because we don't truly know if students will open up to us and tell us the truth about something that they think might hurt our feelings. Jonathan actually prefaced his questions by reminding Jennifer and Roger how much he respected them and that his feelings would not be hurt in any way if they had some criticisms that would make him a better teacher. Take a look at what Jonathan learned about his teaching and his relationships with Jennifer and Roger:

> Mr. Creswell, you are such a cool teacher. You make social studies come alive. When you re-enact stuff and dress up, when you threw the textbook out the window, when you came to my softball game and cheered me on, well, I guess you really are going to be one of those memorable teachers for the rest of my life.
>
> **—Jennifer, Grade 8**

Roger piggybacked on what Jennifer said, but offered a new lens for reflection. By this time, Jonathan was really honored and felt proud of the energy that he expended on a daily basis—and how it was noticed by his students. He liked knowing how much they appreciated his planning, strategizing, and humorous interpretations of historical figures. Notice how Roger provides the feedback necessary for reflective growth—all because Jonathan placed his fears and ego aside and asked his students what they thought about him:

Yeah, you really should have gone into acting, Mr. Creswell. You are so energized and crazy sometimes. We love ya, man, but you know, sometimes, and I mean this with no disrespect, Mr. Creswell, but sometimes, like, well, you go overboard and then we forget that you were talking about the Battle of Gettysburg. You, like, uh, you know, take it too far and I feel like I am at the show. When you do stuff like that once in a while and not every day, you keep us on our toes instead of us just expecting that you are going to do something crazy every single day. Sometimes we want to talk to our friends about it. Sometimes, less of you and more of us is more. You know what I mean?

—Roger, Grade 8

With such powerful input, Roger assisted Jonathan with arriving at a turning point in his career. After all, he knew he was a good teacher, so what Roger said didn't hurt his feelings. He reflected on always being a *sage on the stage* and trying to draw students in with the element of instructional surprise, while also realizing that his daily innovation and acting could get a bit "old" more quickly than he thought.

Examining Plotlines

We respect Jonathan for his courage to go for it! He wanted to seek student voice in his life and in his career. Asking his students for their thoughts and collecting their narratives wasn't as scary as he had expected and he learned he has a better relationship with his students than he thought. The mutual respect that he discovered helped him to reflect about being a sage on the stage. To this day, Jonathan uses the element of surprise to hook students more than getting into a routine of expected acting episodes that might have exhausted his entire class. He even looked into implementing some cooperative learning strategies so he could incorporate more student-to-student dialogue and projects for learning key information. Balance is key for Jonathan, and these stories were delivered to him with love. All he had to do was just ask his students.

The Student Voice Plotline: "We love you, Mr. Creswell. You are an amazing teacher. You excite us, but, don't try so hard. Balance and surprise is OK. We would hate for your talent to become boring to us in the long run. We also like learning from each other and we want to try out being able to perform like you do. I bet we can be entertaining and catch you off guard too."

What We Need to Consider: In what ways can we venture down a path for honest in-your-face feedback that is still respectful from our students? How can student voice transform your world and make you feel good as an educator all at the same time? Can we listen to our students' plotlines and match them with what we think should happen in our classrooms and schools and then consider making adjustments if necessary?

Voice Activator Reflections: Can we place our egos and feelings aside to get the truth from our students about what they really think about what we do each day? How can we establish relationships with our students that will allow them to be honest with us about our teaching? How can we incorporate their respectful feedback into a typical school day?

THE HEALTHY TEACHER AND JOYFUL TEARS

As long as I'm having fun, I'm not quitting.

–Sue Johanson

Jaylen Simms, a tenth-grade biology teacher in New York City, would do anything for her students. She works in a high-poverty school and arrives at work at five o'clock in the morning and leaves at eight o'clock at night. Jaylen plans, eats, sleeps, and breathes for her students. Jaylen is devoted to them and wants to see them succeed so badly that she sometimes blames herself when they fail a test or don't come to school.

Jaylen picks students up at their houses or apartments if she has to, feeds them healthy snacks all day long, and provides a caring environment in her classroom. She is their mom away from home. That's how she characterized herself when speaking with us. Jaylen doesn't have a playground at her school, but she has a garden area with some benches in a tiny courtyard. She regularly chats with her students there because it's a healthy turf. Jaylen asked her students the same questions that Jonathan asked his students from the previous story. She also threw in this question:

What advice do you have for me both as a teacher and as a person?

Jaylen decided to put herself out there. She wanted to know what her students thought. What she found out changed her life forever and maybe even saved her from *herself*.

> Miss Simms, we love you. You saved Reginald from doing something crazy last summer when he got into a fight with Blakely. You helped Tiara to not get thrown out from her house when she got into a fight with her mom's boyfriend. You helped me to stop drinking before school because I hated myself when Owen broke up with me. You keep us alive and we love you. We always will. But my

friends and I want to tell you something. And we mean this with love. You are burning out. We can see it. Your eyes are tired. Your spirit is fading even though you still fight for us. You are losing weight. And we want to save you too. We want to tell you that we need you so badly that we just have to tell you to chill out a bit. Stop coming here so early. Sleep. Stop leaving so late. Do something fun. So my peeps and I bought you something. Here [hands Jaylen a card]. Open it. We got this for you so you can do something nice for yourself. We want you to go get your nails done because they are, like, chewed to the bone. Your nervousness and fatigue are showin' through. [Everyone laughs while Jaylen's eyes well up with tears.] We love you, Miss Simms. We love you so much. But you gotta start taking care of yourself. And who knows? Maybe those new nails will get you a nice boyfriend or something to take your mind off of your worries!

—Denesha, Grade 10

[Jaylen hugs five of her students at once while thanking them with joyful tears.]

Jaylen has printouts of her students' narratives all over her classroom walls. She prides herself in celebrating student voice because it gives her a pick-me-up on even the toughest days. She now knows that when she is broken-hearted because things don't go right or when she beats herself up about something she couldn't control, her students see it in her face. They see her expressions. They get it. Sometimes, they feel sorry for her, and other times they want to grab her by the ears and tell her to shake it off.

Teaching and leading students are emotional jobs, but can we rely on our students to set us straight and splash us in the face with cold water to wake us up? We talked with Jaylen just before finishing our final manuscript for this book because she loved seeing her story in print. It gives her the boost that she needs to carry on and fight on for her students. She lives for the **Let Them Speak!** Project and shares stories with her colleagues who are now also accessing and activating student voice to improve their professions and lives. Going to get her nails done—that simple gift of caring, respect, appreciation, and all-out unconditional love—will stay with Jaylen forever. It is her fight song for her students and for herself. She knows that staying healthy is important to her students. She knows that they cared enough about her to tell her. It was just the cold splash of water on her face that she needed.

TO OUR PRINCIPALS WITH LOVE

Setting goals is the first step in turning the invisible into the visible.

–Tony Robbins

Stories from students and accessing their voices can do wonders for all kinds of school leaders. Sometimes it is more difficult to extract the power of students' voices when a school leader is further removed from the student body or doesn't interact with students on a regular basis. Teachers see their students constantly. This might not be the case with some principals or other administrators, so the challenge of seeking powerful input from students can be greater. Even the best principal on the planet might be lacking knowledge about some of his or her students just because of sheer population size. We believe activating student voice can only ease that challenge.

We might not feel comfortable talking about what we think are important adult issues to our students. But we can. What we think our students could not possibly understand or articulate may very well be what they understand more than we do.

THE LURE OF THE LIBRARY

Consider this story from Joshua, a fifth grader in a rural elementary school in Wyoming, during a time when budget cuts were looming and Principal Kaitlyn Williams was trying to figure out staffing for the upcoming school year.

Kaitlyn sought feedback from her own playground on a gorgeous summer day after the school year was over. She noticed Joshua reading the book *Wonder* on one of the playground swings. She got up from her desk, where she was working on her staffing plan, and walked outside to sit next to Joshua. They started talking about *Wonder* and she asked Joshua these questions:

1. If I was forced to reduce something at our school to save money, what ideas can you give me to make the best decisions possible?
2. What types of programs are important to you at our school?

Prior to visiting Joshua on the playground, Kaitlyn was considering cutting the full-time library media specialist's hours to a part-time schedule and laying off the teacher aide in the library in order to save budget money for the district. But her conversation with Joshua gave her more to consider:

> Mrs. Williams, I'm really loving this book. Auggie, the main character, is so intriguing. The way he is being bullied by the other kids is so sad, but such a great message to teach kids—you know, how bullying is so terrible for kids. You are such a cool principal when you have us take our lessons from the library and decorate the entire school with book posters to get other kids interested in reading. The school is like a great big Amazon page—enticing my

friends to read books that they would never dream of reading. I call it the "lure of the library." But, you know, I still like my Star Wars books too, Mrs. Williams. You can't touch the library, Mrs. Williams. You just can't. That is where you will lose some of us. We depend on the library and Mrs. Friedle. Some kids hate going there, but that's just because they don't like to read. Mrs. Friedle is really so funny. Most of us love going to the library and checking books out even if it is only once a week. But you know what? Why do we have so many monitors in the cafeteria? That's where you can trust us some more by not having so many adults in there. I haven't seen my friends get crazy in there, so why do we need so many adults in there? In fact, how many kids get sent down to you from the cafeteria because of misbehavior?

—Joshua, Grade 5

Joshua was right. Kaitlyn didn't have many problems in the cafeteria. She couldn't remember dealing with much of anything because of the cafeteria, but she wasn't sure if it was because there were a lot of monitors in there or because the kids were just generally well behaved. She decided it was worth looking into. The library cuts started to flee her mind. Maybe Joshua was onto something. Maybe his voice spoke for all 355 students at Kaitlyn's school or it was just one student's voice and opinion. Either way, maybe Joshua was right.

What is most interesting about this story is that Joshua was more valuable than any adult in the district because he had the inside perception and scoop about how the school really operated. Kaitlyn's eyes lit up when she heard what Joshua had to say about issues she honestly didn't expect him to be able to speak to or articulate. But he did, and his insights provided her with incredible information.

As a result, cafeteria monitors were reduced by seventy-five percent, and the library staff was kept intact—all because Kaitlyn looked out her window on a hot July day and reintroduced herself to the most important client and perhaps problem solver on the planet: Joshua, her student.

Examining Plotlines

Kaitlyn chose to speak to Joshua in a way that goes far beyond her typical day-to-day interactions with students, and his story permitted her—and the rest of us—to enter into his private world. Kaitlyn probably knows the most about her school staffing and budget, and she could have chosen to solve the problem on her own. But, she took a leap of faith and asked one of her students for his opinion. While jobs were still lost, the treasure of the school library was saved.

The Student Voice Plotline: "Mrs. Williams, I like how you make reading come alive. You are a great principal. Don't take away our library or teacher who means the world to us. Can't you look at other areas of the school? What about the cafeteria? Do we really need all of those monitors when most students behave pretty well in the cafeteria?"

What We Need to Consider: In what ways might students help us to see our own school programs in ways that we never thought of? How can you take a topic that people don't think belongs to students and make it theirs by asking them what they think?

Voice Activator Reflections: What topics are typically seen as adult issues at your school and how can you discuss them with your students? How can you and your colleagues let your students in on some of the professional challenges you face? Is there something you are working on right now that you haven't thought of sharing with your students but might consider talking over with them?

STEEL KNEES

Gavin Peters, a middle school principal in New Jersey, needed two knee-replacement surgeries, one after the other, during his first year as a principal. He had badly damaged his knees as a baseball catcher in high school and college, and though the need for the surgery was urgent, he was hesitant. Gavin was worried about how much time he would have to take off and how it would affect his job. He was nervous about hobbling around, using the elevator, or trying to maneuver a wheelchair in areas that weren't wheelchair accessible. Gavin truly loved the kids at his school and the playground was one of those special places that he regularly visited to solicit powerful student voices—especially whenever he didn't feel at his best.

One day, during a school-wide end-of-year picnic, Gavin sat on a bench near the playground. Still in a lot of pain after his second surgery, he found himself close to tears even as he watched the kids celebrating. Gavin's recovery was taking a toll on him, and he was struggling to complete the end-of-the-year planning sessions he had scheduled with his team teachers before everyone left for summer vacation. He tried to compose himself, but two of his student ambassadors, Noah, an eighth grader, and Sandy, a seventh grader, ran over to him and sat beside him on the bench. They saw Gavin's face and asked him what was wrong. As he spoke about his pain, he remembered that Sandy had been in and out of the hospital all year long due to a malignant tumor in her neck. She was scheduled to have surgery in order to remove the tumor and start chemotherapy treatments over the summer instead of enjoying some time off like the other kids at her school.

While sitting on the playground bench with Noah and Sandy, Gavin called over to three of his teacher leaders who were relaxing and eating lunch on the grass. These were the three teachers who ran the school-planning team. As Gavin's teachers listened in, Gavin asked Noah and Sandy two questions that changed his life forever:

1. What do you look for in a principal?
2. How can I be a better principal?

Here were their responses:

> You care about us, Mr. Peters, and that's all anyone could ever ask for in a principal. No school is perfect and not all principals are like you, either. You are always around and we never get nervous about "the principal" being around because we always see you. That is the greatest gift you could give any kid—that you care for them so much that you want to see them and learn about what they are learning. You take away the fear of the principal coming around and just to get someone trouble.
>
> **—Noah, Grade 8**

> Yeah, even hobbling around, Mr. Steel Knees! We love you, Mr. Peters. Just get well. Take some time away from the crutches and get well. We want to see you next year, you know [Sandy points to her own neck and gives Mr. Peters a thumbs-up].
>
> **—Sandy, Grade 7**

From that point on, Gavin Peters was known as Gavin "Steel Knees" Peters. The questions didn't give Gavin the outcome he hoped for. It gave him more—the spirit to continue caring for his students, no matter what kind of pain he would ever face in life. He didn't receive good ideas about programming or instructional goals for the following school year. He received care from his students— which is exactly what Gavin needed at *that* specific moment during *that* specific day of the school year. He connected to his students on a deeply personal level and was reminded that relationships drive all outcomes. For Gavin, Noah, and Sandy, the loving respect that they shared with one another could never be compared to letter grades or percentiles. It's simply what makes the world go around.

Examining Plotlines

These stories do something powerful and magical. They offer glimpses into the souls and minds of our students—things we never thought they thought about or felt about us. Sometimes we have no idea how much students appreciate us. We don't go around looking for accolades to boost our egos, but we are humans too, and we love when others make us feel good.

The Student Voice Plotline: "I am glad that you are my teacher. I am glad that you are my principal. I spend a lot of time with you, and I know how hard you work. You do so much for me. Sometimes you clothe me and feed me. You teach me, of course, but not just English and math. You teach me about life. You are like a second mom or dad to me. I need you more than you even know and I don't tell you how much I appreciate you because sometimes I feel weird. You know, I respect you and don't want you to think I'm corny or anything. But you really have left your mark on me. I'll never forget you. Ever. Thank you."

What We Need to Consider: In what ways do stories, such as these, get lost or forgotten? How can these stories motivate us to be even better the next day? Perhaps these stories can even provide comfort when we feel lost in our own careers or when we feel as if no one is getting what we are saying. We need a boost just like everyone else—like when our lessons flop or our paperwork overwhelms us.

Voice Activator Reflections: Try being vulnerable enough to ask your students what they like and don't like about you. Consider asking them for advice, and encourage them to commit healthy treason in your classroom. What are some ways that you can keep your mind open for the human spirit and ask your students to be vulnerable too? Those are the episodes that keep us going. They are the spirit and lifeline of education. They provide us with the resolve to get up in the morning and do "it" all over again.

Most teachers have been there—feeling unappreciated, overworked, and desperate for something to make it better. We believe that our students and their voices can rejuvenate and transform us. We just have to muster the courage to ask them what they think. Let's renew our commitment to doing whatever it takes to make us better educators.

TO OUR DISTRICT-WIDE LEADERS WITH LOVE

The Freshman Academy

While some of the narratives throughout this book altered the course of a classroom, grade level, or school, this narrative affected a district, which permeated an entire state. The most connected and impactful district leaders skillfully seek out and listen for community voice, family voice, teacher voice, and student voice. The role of district administrators typically doesn't require frontline instructional interaction with students directly (even though the decisions they make directly impact the daily lives of our students). By mere job design, district administrators tend to be consumed with leading curriculum, instruction, assessment, home-to-school communications, extracurricular activities, lunch programs, and community relations using every data bank imaginable to monitor the success of their programs! For district leaders, these banks of data—absenteeism, free and reduced lunch rates, the number of students exiting ELL programs, interim assessments, state assessments, and graduation rates—are closely monitored because they must follow state and federal demands. There is no getting around these kinds of job requirements. The good news is that voice-activating leaders look far beyond compliance to analyze the trends that lead to meeting all of the needs of our students.

We contend that voice activators are accountable for student success, which extends far beyond student-achievement outcomes. Voice activators believe in Maslow before Bloom because they seek to meet the needs of the whole child. Impactful, far-reaching leaders push boundaries by listening for ways to support student behavior, social-emotional aspects of human interactions, and ways to inspire and impact academic growth.

In the Cabot Public School District in Arkansas, district and school administrators meet quarterly to collaborate on their district-wide data. Although data is the ultimate driving force behind their discussions, the focus is always about making things better for students. Back in 2013, the district leadership team met to reflect on their current performance. During this meeting, Superintendent Dr. Tony Thurman drew their attention to the high school dropout rate that had been on the rise for the previous three years.

As a leadership team of district administrators and principals, they continued the dropout rate conversation. The group came to a consensus that they needed to identify the grade level from which students were jumping ship. After looking at the historical trends, they uncovered that a high percentage of students were dropping out of school during the first semester of their sophomore year in one particular high school that served grades ten through twelve.

Dr. Thurman posed the following questions to his leadership team:

1. What is happening during sophomore year that makes these kids want to quit?
2. What is happening with the transition from junior high to high school?

The team members looked around the room inquisitively, and a few even shrugged their shoulders. Dr. Thurman insisted that they must get to the bottom of this district-wide problem immediately. He asked that they pull a list of students who had recently dropped out in order to analyze their data even more closely. He wondered if there was an underlying cause—poverty, race, gender, or something else—that the adults just couldn't pinpoint. He knew that there had to be a reason, and if his team could pinpoint that reason, it would curb a problematic trend.

After coming back together to analyze test scores and class programming, the district leadership team couldn't put their finger on any one factor that was contributing to the upward trend of an increasing dropout rate. At the end of the meeting, Dr. Thurman leaned forward over the table, with both hands gripping the edges of it, and said to his district administrative team, "Well, I'm going to have to sit down with those kids myself and let them speak and find out what they think!"

And he did. He called the high school to find out the time period when his sophomores met for lunch in the cafeteria, and he devoted an entire week to hanging out with his students in order to ask them what he could do to improve the high school experience so everyone would have the drive and desire to graduate. Look at what Dr. Thurman discovered through his discussions with his students:

It's really hard once you get behind in one class. If you fail a class, then there isn't really a way to make it up. You have to start the class all over again the next semester, but then that means that you have to cut out another class and it is just too hard to recover enough credits to graduate. I wish there was someone who could help us once we get behind.

—Betty May, Grade 10

I mean look at this place, it's like a maze. I'm already scared of the juniors and seniors looking down at me and I feel stupid asking for directions to get to the bathroom or the library. That is just asking for it. If students knew how to get to their classes or even just where to find the bathrooms the first day of school, that would have made a difference. I was so scared the first week of school because I had no clue where to go. Honestly, I didn't want to come back, but I had my mom breathing down my neck and telling me to get to school!

—Tristan, Grade 10

It is hard enough being a teenager with friends, but when you throw us into a high school where we don't know any of the teachers and there are tons of students in our own grade level that we don't know, this place is intimidating. I just want to sit in the back and count down the minutes until the day is over. It's one thing if you are in a safe environment where you know everyone. It's another when you are just a number. I say if you really want to make this place better, then we gotta work on creating relationships or at least put us in classes with the students we knew last year.

—Gabby, Grade 10

If you really want to know, my home life is tough. Okay it is more than tough, it sucks. My mom is on disability in a wheelchair, my dad is still in jail, and my uncle lost his job and is sleeping on our couch in the front room of the trailer. I'm the one everyone depends on to make sure my mom gets her medicine and my little sister gets to school. When it comes down to it, school is the last thing on my mind. I'm just living day to day trying to make sure my family is taken care of, especially my sister. If I had time to make up my tests and catch up, I would, but the reality is from the time I arrive at home after school and leave in the morning, I'm just putting out fires and taking care of everyone. I don't even have friends of my own to talk to. There isn't time to do anything else. Believe it or not, I actually like school because it is the one place that I can be a kid instead of an adult. I wish I could do both, but I can't. Some days I don't even want to live. It isn't that I don't want to finish school, it's that I don't stand a chance. It wasn't the cards I was dealt. Aside from winning the lottery and healing my mom and getting my dad out of jail, there's really nothing you can do to make school better. I don't blame you. I really don't even know who to blame, I just know it isn't for me anymore.

—Kimmi Ann, Grade 10

Listening to this group of students and hearing each individual story was more than Dr. Thurman had expected. It was eye opening, gut wrenching, and even stung a little. He knew that action needed to be taken to ensure that every student who enrolled in his district was guaranteed equity and a voice. As difficult as it was to hear these stories and more, it was worth taking the time to listen to each and every story.

After talking with more than thirty students over the course of one week, Dr. Thurman noticed several common themes:

1. Students were honest—even brutally honest at times.
2. Students wanted to be heard. They wanted to share their stories.
3. When students failed a class, they got further and further behind. Many decided it was too hard to recover, and it wasn't worth staying in school. For those students, credit recovery felt like an impossible feat.
4. For many students, the transition to high school was an anxiety attack waiting to happen because it was a huge building. Students didn't know where rooms were located in relation to the bathrooms, gym, and cafeteria or to which wing of the school they were in. The campus was large, and students needed personalized tours in order to be able to get around starting on the very first day of school.
5. The transition to high school was emotionally traumatic for many students because they were bombarded with a new social dynamic. On top of feeling awkward about a new school, they didn't know many of the students or teachers. They were also thrown into a schedule where they had to self-direct their entire days without the support of power-ful mentorships.
6. Poverty, trauma, and life circumstances often negatively impacted the possibility for students to be successful in a traditional school setting.

Never satisfied with the status quo, Dr. Thurman assembled his team once again to figure out how to prevent the need for credit recovery, help students navigate the physical space of their school, assist with transitioning, and provide a nurturing environment with trusted relationships that would meet every student where they were with no exceptions. Dr. Thurman took this as a personal challenge and internalized and wrestled with these issues while mulling it over for weeks until he could figure out how to shake things up.

One day it hit him and Dr. Thurman had an idea. A radical idea. He knew that he must share his idea with others. He shouted over with a resonating bellow to his administrative secretary, "Hey Karen . . . set up a meeting for tomorrow afternoon with my team so we can discuss the dropout rates. Make sure they know that this meeting is mandatory. It's *that* important."

The following morning, Dr. Thurman led a discussion with decisive, assertive, and passionate prowess. He stood pondering for a moment, and everyone was captivated by the intensity in the room and the suspense of him calling a last-minute meeting. Dr. Thurman enthusiastically said:

> I want to share some of the stories that I heard this past week. I wrote them down, and they are on your handout if you want to follow along. It is crystal clear to me that we've got to make this right. The words of these students have been swirling around in my mind, and finally it hit me. I've got an idea that I think may work: What if we started a freshman academy? Now hear me out—it would be a smaller version of the high school, so the layout would be the same. We would focus on team building and relationships of students so they felt a sense of family and community without the fear of the upperclassman. And we would monitor their grades and progress even more closely and provide interventions and tutoring to ensure

that they are on target for graduation before they even come to high school. We will do whatever it takes to make sure they are taken care of as a family.

Looking at the faces of his administrative team, you could have read a blinking neon sign running across their faces that screamed, Come again? You want to do what? After all, it was an unconventional response—it wasn't the type of data that they were used to. Dr. Thurman's progressive idea transpired because he believed in the power behind student voice and student narratives while being brave and vulnerable enough to ask his students what they thought about dropout rates. Dr. Thurman was a true voice activator at work.

After the shock value wore off and dialogue about the Freshman Academy continued, ideas started to evolve, and passionate conversations about purposeful planning illuminated the room. No longer was this an idea on the table: The Cabot Public Schools Freshman Academy was born.

ALL IN

The Freshman Academy opened its doors to the community in the fall of 2014 under the leadership of principal Tanya Spillane. Prior to their grand opening, there was much planning and logistical preparations taking place behind the scenes. This newly appointed principal, along with a team of new teachers, didn't waste a single minute in establishing their mission and goals for their Freshman Academy. Take a look at how they designed their mission:

MISSION STATEMENT

To establish and showcase a learning environment that will provide programs and supports that will address the unique needs of freshman transitioning to a high school setting. Goals will include...

- Increasing student achievement with higher grade-point averages and decreasing the number of students who fail to obtain full credits in ninth grade.
- Increasing student attendance.
- Decreasing student discipline incidents.
- Encouraging student involvement in school activities and functions.
- Aiding with social transition to the high school environment.
- Establishing positive connections and transitions for incoming ninth-grade students with a specific set of teachers.
- Providing early identification and interventions for at-risk behaviors.
- Increasing class identity and cohesiveness.

IT IS ALL ABOUT RELATIONSHIPS

Without human connectivity and knowing our *why* and living our *why*, everything is an automated response Goals will include ... and teaching becomes a job. To be effective educators, we must not only know our *why*, we must have the skillset to help students find their *why* for learning. High school poses a particular challenge as the demand for independence increases. Students are more distracted, responsibilities are increased, and the cognitive demands for learning can be stressful. Relationships are the conduit to everything.

While in the planning stages of this new academy, Principal Spillane took the time to visit other high schools and read books and articles while furiously soaking up anything that would set the course of success for this new district model. She was passionate about monitoring students' academic progress to ensure every student left the academy on target for graduation and, more importantly, that each and every student felt a sense of belonging. She knew it was time to roll up her sleeves and develop a strategic plan with her team.

PLCS AND C2G

Principal Spillane was adamant about establishing professional learning communities (PLCs) for teachers and students. Once a week, teams of teachers (not only exclusive to content area or subject-area departments) met to discuss student success, trends from teacher to teacher, and students who were failing or were significantly behind in their work. This was not a planning session for content and lesson plans; this was a PLC to talk about student success. Within any type of large school, it is very easy to get lost in a sea of students rather than to develop meaningful relationships on a student-to-student basis, especially in high school. Developing PLCs by teaming teachers together was an integral part of her plan to monitor student success in terms of setting up achievement goals and a sense of belonging to a community. Every student was analyzed as a whole child with a focus on teacher collaboration in order to set targets for graduation.

Another idea that was conceived as a response to garnering student voice was their Commitment to Graduate Program (C2G). They developed a time during the day for a walk-to-intervention hybrid model. Since many of the Freshman Academy students participate, in multiple clubs and extracurricular activities that kept them out late nearly every night of the week, they knew students did not have ample time at home to study and keep up with their academic demands. These high-performing students could easily lag behind in their academics if they lacked the time in the evening to complete homework or properly study for their exams. They were reliant on a teacher coming before or after school (or even during a teacher's lunch time) to help students. Those time periods didn't always work. A school-wide time designated during the day to allow students to sit with teachers during this C2G time to simply make up a test or to get extra support in a content area that they were not grasping, this additional element of the academy was born. This was a need for not only high-achieving students who were overconsumed with extra-curricular activities, but also for those who had a more challenging home life. It was a win/win situation for everyone.

During C2G time, students who were on target with grades and assignments had the freedom of choice to spend time as they pleased. They could go to the gym to play sports, the cafeteria to lounge or visit with their friends, the music room to practice, or the library to grab a book or use their laptop or tablets. The teaming approach didn't always come easy, and staff members had to set up a system for monitoring students in each space with appropriate supervision.

GIVE ME FIVE LIFESAVERS

As a hands-on principal, Tanya Spillane, her administrative team, and teachers knew every student by name. They knew their students' plights and personal stories. At the beginning of the school year, there were over eighty-five students who had failed one or more courses in junior high. As an administrative team, Principal Spillane created a folder for every one of those eighty-five students and doled them out evenly among the school leadership team members. The expectation was that they would meet with their "folder" students on a regular basis to check in on their lives and get to know their stories. Every time they met, they were to capture something that made that student light up, whether it was talking about their dog, Buster; their grandpa who lived in another state; or their passion or enjoyment of a sport or a television show. Something new would be learned to strengthen relationships. They were also expected to dialogue with their students in order to identify any possible barriers that they might be facing.

One day, during PLC team meetings, Principal Spillane stopped by one group of teachers during their regular team meeting. She brought index cards with her and posed a challenge. She said, "I'm giving you each an index card and on that card I want you to each write down five students whom you don't know all that well. Before the next time we meet, I want you to share with me what you learned about that student you didn't know before and how you bridged a relationship to learn their story."

The teachers worked together, each writing down different student names and committing to the challenge. The following week, Principal Spillane checked in with this teacher group again and asked them to share what they had learned about their five students. In an honest confessional tone, one teacher spoke up and said, "To be honest, grades were due, and I was behind on grading, and I had parents to call, we had soccer playoffs, and I just couldn't fit it all in. I know it is important, and I still think it is important, but time was an issue." This teacher was honest and Principal Spillane valued his honesty, so she set up the same challenge for the following week.

The next week, Principal Spillane showed up to the meeting, again, but now holding a bag of Lifesavers. She asked the teachers to take out their index cards consisting of the names of five kids in order to share what they learned about each student. One teacher shared that because she bridged a relationship, that student now arrives early to class just to talk to her and another student stops by after football practice just to visit. Principal Spillane reached into her bag of Lifesavers and placed exactly five pieces of candy on that particular teacher's desk and said:

> I am giving you Lifesavers to give away. But you cannot give away your Lifesaver to a new student until you bridge a relationship that made a difference. To the two students who now seek you out because of an authentic relationship that you have developed, give them their Lifesavers. You see, it isn't about you (the teacher), it's about what you pour into each student. Once you form a relationship, then you can make a difference. Teaching is more than content; it is more than interventions. It is about getting to know kids on a personal level to "life save" them.

Students now leave Freshman Academy as a family with all of the credits that they need to be on target in order to be successful in high school. As a result, Cabot's dropout rate was drastically reduced.

Actively seeking student voice doesn't end with teachers or school-based leaders; it is a living, breathing practice that can transform an entire community. Listening for pivot points can lead to a path of improvement when followed by a leader-driven community action.

To this day, the physical replica of the layout of the high school—a miniature academy version in Cabot—helps students to get the lay of the land, find a sense of belonging, and be academically on target for graduation. Student voice has transformed a community. Student voice compelled a district-wide leader to follow the intuitions and realities of words that will forever be remembered.

Examining the Plotlines

Structures can be set up in the name of student voice. Entire communities can benefit from what students say.

The Student Voice Plotline: "Relationships matter more than anything. If you take the time to get to know me, I will do anything in the world for you. If you really want to know what we think, we will tell you, but you might not like the answers. I can't believe you had no clue that high school is so emotionally disturbing for us. We might fake it to look cool or because we don't want to be thrown into a locker. But high school is pretty scary. We want help. How about asking us how to make it better? Thanks for taking the time to know me. Thanks for making sure that I do not become a dropout casualty. Thank you for caring about me as a person, first, and as a student, second."

What We Need to Consider: Some structures within our schools feel enormous, and existing practices and policies often feel like a beast that can never truly be tackled, but we have to be bold enough to examine all that we do. It might seem risky, but we must seek out student feedback and input on the rules, procedures, and functions that affect them the most.

Voice Activator Reflections: How many students have you gotten to know? What are some practices in your classroom or school that need to audit on a regular basis? What's something you've always wanted to just ask your students? How can you activate student voice in response to negative trends—or to keep positive trends going—at your school? How will you let them speak?

We can either embrace student voice or brace ourselves for failure.

When we fail ourselves, we will fail our students.

Opening the window to student voice is the fresh air of spring that clears out a musty room.

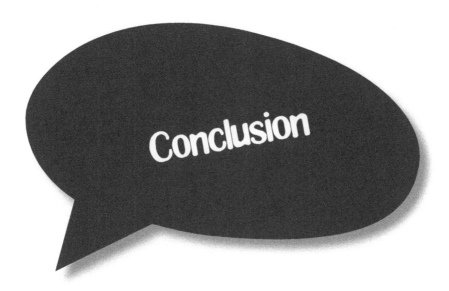

Conclusion

Vulnerability is not a weakness, rather it is our most accurate measurement of courage and the birthplace of innovation, creativity, and change.

—Brené Brown

PLAYING THE RECORDER?

Zach, a fourth grader in Rochester, New York, was given a musical recorder instrument to play just like all of his fourth-grade classmates. When he looked at the recorder, he blew into it once, then he shook his head, and while no one was looking during free time, he proceeded to hide the instrument on the highest shelf in a cupboard located in his classroom so no one could find it. When it was "recorder time" each week, his music teacher, Regina Tompkins, asked Zach why he didn't have his recorder with him—why he was repeatedly unprepared. He said that he lost it and would try to find it for next week's class. This went on for three weeks until Zach finally *got into trouble* for being unprepared. He had to go to the principal's office. Some of Zach's friends would talk about how much they hated the recorder. Yet, others loved playing the instrument! So, what was going on with Zach?

One day, Zach's classroom teacher, Marsha Zellings, was looking for some math kits and looked in the very same cabinet where Zach hid his recorder. Finding the hidden treasure with Zach's name labeled on the case, Mrs. Zellings had a talk with Zach. She wanted to know why he had hidden his instrument while telling Miss Tompkins that he had lost it. Here is what Zach had to say:

> I . . . I don't want to play that. I want to be a drummer. Why do we all have to play the same thing? I hate the recorder. Doesn't this school need at least one drummer? I've got rhythm, you know, Mrs. Z.!
>
> **—Zach, Grade 4**

Instead of fighting with Zach in order to have him conform with participating in a recorder army, Mrs. Zellings actually listened to his concerns and agreed with him. She met with Miss Tompkins, and as a result, the school no longer mandated recorders for every single fourth grader. To this day, music has been reconfigured, replanned, and renovated for the students. Rhythm instruments, wind instruments, and other types of offerings were given to the fourth graders to try out. And those who didn't want to play an instrument didn't have to. They have alternative activities, such as STEM-building classes to replace musical mandates.

You might be thinking that it is a good thing to expose students to the recorder—to try to instill a love of music and music appreciation. But, at what expense are we not servicing our students when we decide, as adults, that everyone is going to do the same exact thing in the same exact way? If Zach hadn't spoken up, and if his teachers hadn't truly wanted to listen to his voice, the recorder would have continued to be a way of life for the rest of every student's life for the eternity of school as they know it in Zach's simple music class.

STUDENT VOICE = DATA

In *Moneyball*, the movie based on the book by Michael Lewis, Billy Beane, the general manager of the Oakland A's, (portrayed by Brad Pitt) had an epiphany: Baseball's conventional wisdom was all wrong. Faced with a tight budget, Beane had to reinvent his team by outsmarting the richer ball clubs. Joining forces with Ivy League graduate Peter Brand, (played by Jonah Hill), Beane began to challenge the game's old-school traditions. He recruited bargain-bin players whom the scouts labeled as "flawed," but still had game-winning potential.

Beane and Brand used batting data, other player stats, and mathematic formulas to rethink their biases about what it takes to build a winning baseball team. They used statistics to find value in players that no one else could see. The code that was written to analyze players through the eye of mathematics used statistics to include all of the intelligence that could be used to build a winning team that would get more hits and RBI's. The coaching staff overlooked players for a variety of biased reasons due to their perceived flaws. Check out this clip here: youtu.be/yGf6LNWY9AI.

Student voice is the game-changing data that we are missing in education. It will take all of your knowledge, expertise, opinions, and perceptions to bend what you think you might know, push you to know, and transform you to know for new identities as teachers, school leaders, and educators of all kinds who can create winning schools. Student voice can be more powerful than any data, numbers, or trends because it brings to life the *human element* that is often missing in our schools. Student voice will make you aware of real-life problems and choices that you didn't know existed. It will give you new issues to reckon with. But this is a good kind of reckoning. It can be fun, empowering, and incredibly emotional, but it is exceedingly important work that we must roll our sleeves up and access each day. To better serve our students, we must create schools where students who speak up and use their voices loudly are more cherished than the test scores that we use to label and sort them.

With every stone that you turn over in the name of accessing and activating student voice, shout out to others what you have learned. Remember, if student voice does not provide new insights about an issue, that's okay too. Sometimes the power of student voice is found in simply validating something that we might already be doing.

In our own work, we are grateful for the expertise and guidance of Isaiah Sterling, who provided insight and recommended changes and contributions to the authenticity of this book with his own powerful student voice! We thank the STEAM girls from Hamilton High School in Arizona for demonstrating the importance of their voices and stories. We challenge you to put yourself on the line and break *The Eight Comfort Zones* outlined in the final section of this book below.

One Final Voice Activator Reflection: We are not trying to hypnotize you, but just say this out loud ten times in a row, and it will be yours forever:

"Let Them Speak!" . . . *"Let Them Speak!"* . . . Now, eight more times, please . . .

The couch can be a warm place. It can be a comfortable place.

But what if the answers to what you are looking for are somewhere outside?

What if we asked you to get off the couch?

THE EIGHT COMFORT ZONES

Metaphorically speaking, there are so many daily events or daily activities that we conform to. If we are used to doing something the same way, how will we ever know if victory awaits us if we do it differently or "**Bass A**kwards?" Take a look at some common activities below as we wonder what *uncomfortability* might look like in your classroom or school.

1. Fumble the ball on purpose:

What if a running back stopped the play on the field and held out the football for the other team to grab? It's kind of funny to think about, but we are all on the same team, even when competition exists. Do you currently turn over your classroom or school to your students? No, we mean *really* turn it over—not just on the surface, but deeper. It's a new lens for everything that goes on in your school and everything that you do. We don't mean a *Lord of the Flies* turnover, but turning over what you think is working well to get new insights in a safe, caring environment that matters. We will ask you again: Are you going to *really* turn over your classroom or school to your students, especially when you think things are already going well?

2. Give your students magnifying glasses and decoder rings:

Are you going to let go and do what you do best while asking students what they might know best? See, our kids know things that we don't. They see things that we don't see. They have insights that we would never think of. Our students are like magnifying glasses and decoder rings. If you feel like your expertise is threatened, good. Give them the tools to look more deeply into every nook and cranny of the school instead of being satisfied with that which is *invisible*.

3. Break the speed limit and try something new:

Don't get a speeding ticket, but challenge yourself to not let this opportunity go! Nike running shoes might help you to run faster, but Nike, the goddess from Greek mythology, had wings too, and wings will take you further. You can access and activate student voice now, both quickly and victoriously. In one particular episode of *Seinfeld*, George Costanza started doing the exact opposite thing for every intention that he would typically think was right. Instead of ordering a tuna sandwich on toast and a cup of coffee at the diner like he usually did, he ordered chicken salad on rye with a cup of tea. That's when things started to go *right* for him. Now that's a reflective victory!

4. Walk the walk farther than usual.

Your inner voice is telling you to tap into your students' voices, so why not listen? You know you want to try it. You say, "Kids first," but do you mean it? We believe you if you really do mean it. It's time to walk the walk with us because words are fine, but actions speak volumes. Now this time, walk one mile, but add another two miles to that. Be uncomfortable. Push yourself.

5. Wipe your lenses dirty.

Notice we are asking you to wipe something *dirty*, not *clean*. Student voice will wipe your lenses dirty. It is supposed to be dirty. It is time to refocus your lenses on everything you do in your classroom, school, and community by getting dirty.

6. Flip a coin. Roll the dice. Take a chance.

Think of what the payoff might mean. Sometimes the rewards outweigh the risks!

7. Use funnel-shaped devices where noise is shunned.

A megaphone is used to amplify voices. Go buy one for your classroom or school as a symbol of accessing and activating student voice. "Loud and clear" is crucial for everyone's growth.

8. Change to: Don't let others "chicken out."

"What . . . are you . . . chicken?" said Biff to Marty McFly in the movie *Back to the Future*. We invite you to convince others to join the *Let Them Speak!* Project. If you can't convince them this way, try another tactic and double-dog dare them with a smile. Now, that's breaking the comfort barrier!

The Legacy Speaks!

This book is also dedicated to a warrior of equity, hope, and love:
Principal Tanya Spillane

Principal Spillane was an educator who believed that a student's story should never be judged by the chapter that you've walked in on. She lived her life believing that we meet every student where they are and we need to be free of judging our children at all times.

When we encounter challenging students, it is our job to look beyond their behaviors and figure out why they are acting out or acting peculiarly. Principal Spillane exemplified leadership, community, resilience, and purpose. She will be dearly missed in this earthly life as her legacy will live on for generations to come.

Thank you, Principal Spillane, for your fearless servant leadership to countless numbers of students and staff members whose lives you touched. You will forever be a Cabot Panther, leading through high expectations, excellence, and heartfelt leadership. You "let your students speak" and this is the greatest gift that any educator can give to our youth. We are proud of everything that you worked so hard for in your incredible career; you will always be remembered.

A Call to Action

We invite you to include the ***Let Them Speak!*** Project at your advocacy group, student organization, youth group, or school, starting right now. This book is meant to cultivate you, your classroom, and your school into an army of educators who know that student voice is important and who can also meet our challenge of moving out of comfort zones. With or without us, we challenge you to become voice activators if you are not already fully activated. This is a belief not a program, a practice that honors students as stakeholders. Ask, narrativize, and share the ***Let Them Speak!*** Project is put into action. If you want to improve what you are doing the secret lies within offering exceptional customer service by letting students speak.

Go grab a bag of Skittles and head out to *their* turf.

Bring the Let Them Speak! Project to Your School or Organization

Learn more about data collection processes, engaging stakeholders in the process, how student-centered changes can impact your school. The project is ongoing and Rebecca and Rick would love to share their stories collected. If you are looking to infuse this innovative approach in your school and would like support planning and training staff, don't hesitate to contact them While they are certainly busy activating this movement in schools all across the nation, they are never too busy to come to you and demonstrate the exciting ways that student voice can transform your school. They specialize in all stakeholder groups especially parents, school assemblies to activate Let Them Speak! initiative. If you still are not a believer, you ain't seen nothing yet! We hope that students are the catalyst for this global initiative as social justice warriors! Wait until you hear about the newest transformations that schools are making because educators are accessing and activating student voice!

Reach out and share your narratives and stories of success that resulted from the Let Them Speak! Project:

rebeccacoda1@gmail.com
drjetter1@gmail.com

Let them help your student organization, advocacy group, agency, or parent organization so that everyone has an equitable voice for change. Talk to them about your effort to transform your classroom or school, or simply share your stories with them at the hashtag #LetStudentsSpeak on Twitter.

Visit LetThemSpeak.net and download
100 Prompts for Activating Student Voice.

More from

DAVE BURGESS
Consulting, Inc.

Teach Like a PIRATE

Increase Student Engagement, Boost Your Creativity, and Transform Your Life as an Educator

By Dave Burgess (@BurgessDave)

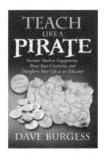

New York Times' bestseller *Teach Like a PIRATE* sparked a worldwide educational revolution with its passionate teaching manifesto and dynamic student-engagement strategies. Translated into multiple languages, it sparks outrageously creative lessons and life-changing student experiences.

P is for PIRATE

Inspirational ABC's for Educators

By Dave and Shelley Burgess (@Burgess_Shelley)

In *P is for Pirate,* husband-and-wife team Dave and Shelley Burgess tap personal experiences of seventy educators to inspire others to create fun and exciting places to learn. It's a wealth of imaginative and creative ideas that makes learning and teaching more fulfilling than ever before.

The Innovator's Mindset

Empower Learning, Unleash Talent, and Lead a Culture of Creativity

By George Couros (@gcouros)

In *The Innovator's Mindset*, teachers and administrators discover that compliance to a scheduled curriculum hinders student innovation, critical thinking, and creativity. To become forward-thinking leaders, students must be empowered to wonder and explore.

Pure Genius

Building a Culture of Innovation and Taking 20% Time to the Next Level

By Don Wettrick (@DonWettrick)

Collaboration—with experts, students, and other educators—helps create interesting and even life-changing opportunities for learning. In *Pure Genius*, Don Wettrick inspires and equips educators with a systematic blueprint for beating classroom boredom and teaching innovation.

Learn Like a PIRATE

Empower Your Students to Collaborate, Lead, and Succeed

By Paul Solarz (@PaulSolarz)

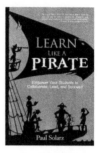

Passing grades don't equip students for life and career responsibilities. *Learn Like a PIRATE* shows how risk-taking and exploring passions in stimulating, motivating, supportive, self-directed classrooms creates students capable of making smart, responsible decisions on their own.

Ditch That Textbook

Free Your Teaching and Revolutionize Your Classroom

By Matt Miller (@jmattmiller)

Ditch That Textbook creates a support system, toolbox, and manifesto that can free teachers from outdated textbooks. Miller empowers them to untether themselves, throw out meaningless, pedestrian teaching and learning practices, and evolve and revolutionize their classrooms.

50 Things You Can Do with Google Classroom

By Alice Keeler and Libbi Miller
(@alicekeeler, @MillerLibbi)

50 Things You Can Do with Google Classroom provides a thorough overview of this GAfE app and shortens the teacher learning curve for introducing technology in the classroom. Keeler and Miller's ideas, instruction, and screenshots help teachers go digital with this powerful tool.

50 Things to Go Further with Google Classroom

A Student-Centered Approach

By Alice Keeler and Libbi Miller
(@alicekeeler, @MillerLibbi)

In *50 Things to Go Further with Google Classroom: A Student-Centered Approach*, authors and educators Alice Keeler and Libbi Miller help teachers create a digitally rich, engaging, student-centered environment that taps the power of individualized learning using Google Classroom.

140 Twitter Tips for Educators

Get Connected, Grow Your Professional Learning Network, and Reinvigorate Your Career

By Brad Currie, Billy Krakower, and Scott Rocco
(@bradmcurrie, @wkrakower, @ScottRRocco)

In *140 Twitter Tips for Educators*, #Satchat hosts and founders of Evolving Educators, Brad Currie, Billy Krakower, and Scott Rocco, offer step-by-step instruction on Twitter basics and building an online following within Twitter's vibrant network of educational professionals.

Master the Media

How Teaching Media Literacy Can Save Our Plugged-In World

By Julie Smith (@julnilsmith)

Master the Media explains media history, purpose, and messaging so teachers and parents can empower students with critical-thinking skills which lead to informed choices, the ability to differentiate between truth and lies, and discern perception from reality. Media literacy can save the world.

The Zen Teacher

Creating Focus, Simplicity, and Tranquility in the Classroom

By Dan Tricarico (@thezenteacher)

Unrushed and fully focused, teachers influence—even improve—the future when they maximize performance and improve their quality of life. In *The Zen Teacher*, Dan Tricarico offers practical, easy-to-use techniques to develop a non-religious Zen practice and thrive in the classroom.

eXPlore Like a Pirate

Gamification and Game-Inspired Course Design to Engage, Enrich, and Elevate Your Learners

By Michael Matera (@MrMatera)

Create an experiential, collaborative, and creative world with classroom game designer and educator Michael Matera's game-based learning book, *eXPlore Like a Pirate*. Matera helps teachers apply motivational gameplay techniques and enhance curriculum with gamification strategies.

Your School Rocks . . . So Tell People!

Passionately Pitch and Promote the Positives Happening on Your Campus

By Ryan McLane and Eric Lowe (@McLane_Ryan, @EricLowe21)

Your School Rocks . . . So Tell People! helps schools create effective social media communication strategies that keep students' families and the community connected to what's going on at school, offering more than seventy immediately actionable tips with easy-to-follow instructions and video tutorial links.

Play Like a Pirate

Engage Students with Toys, Games, and Comics

By Quinn Rollins (@jedikermit)

In *Play Like a Pirate*, Quinn Rollins offers practical, engaging strategies and resources that make it easy to integrate fun into your curriculum. Regardless of grade level, serious learning can be seriously fun with inspirational ideas that engage students in unforgettable ways.

The Classroom Chef

Sharpen Your Lessons. Season Your Classes. Make Math Meaningful

By John Stevens and Matt Vaudrey
(@Jstevens009, @MrVaudrey)

With imagination and preparation, every teacher can be *The Classroom Chef* using John Stevens and Matt Vaudrey's secret recipes, ingredients, and tips that help students "get" math. Use ideas as-is, or tweak to create enticing educational meals that engage students.

How Much Water Do We Have?

5 Success Principles for Conquering Any Challenge and Thriving in Times of Change

By Pete Nunweiler with Kris Nunweiler

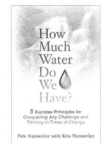

Stressed out, overwhelmed, or uncertain at work or home? It could be figurative dehydration.

How Much Water Do We Have? identifies five key elements necessary for success of any goal, life transition, or challenge. Learn to find, acquire, and use the 5 Waters of Success.

The Writing on the Classroom Wall

How Posting Your Most Passionate Beliefs about Education Can Empower Your Students, Propel Your Growth, and Lead to a Lifetime of Learning

By Steve Wyborney (@SteveWyborney)

Big ideas lead to deeper learning, but they don't have to be profound to have profound impact. Teacher Steve Wyborney explains why and how sharing ideas sharpens and refines them. It's okay if some ideas fall off the wall; what matters most is sharing and discussing.

Kids Deserve It!

Pushing Boundaries and Challenging Conventional Thinking

By Todd Nesloney and Adam Welcome
(@TechNinjaTodd, @awelcome)

Think big. Make learning fun and meaningful. *Kids Deserve It!* Nesloney and Welcome offer high-tech, high-touch, and highly engaging practices that inspire risk-taking and shake up the status quo on behalf of your students. Rediscover why you became an educator, too!

LAUNCH

Using Design Thinking to Boost Creativity and Bring Out the Maker in Every Student

By John Spencer and A.J. Juliani (@spencerideas, @ajjuliani)

When students identify themselves as makers, inventors, and creators, they discover powerful problem-solving and critical-thinking skills. Their imaginations and creativity will shape our future. John Spencer and A.J. Juliani's *LAUNCH* process dares you to innovate and empower them.

Instant Relevance

Using Today's Experiences to Teach Tomorrow's Lessons

By Denis Sheeran (@MathDenisNJ)

Learning sticks when it's relevant to students. In *Instant Relevance,* author and keynote speaker Denis Sheeran equips you to create engaging lessons *from* experiences and events that matter to students while helping them make meaningful connections between the real world and the classroom.

Escaping the School Leader's Dunk Tank

How to Prevail When Others Want to See You Drown

By Rebecca Coda and Rick Jetter
(@RebeccaCoda, @RickJetter)

Dunk-tank situations—discrimination, bad politics, revenge, or ego-driven coworkers—can make an educator's life miserable. Coda and Jetter (dunk-tank survivors themselves) share real-life stories and insightful research to equip school leaders with tools to survive and, better yet, avoid getting "dunked."

Start. Right. Now.

Teach and Lead for Excellence

By Todd Whitaker, Jeff Zoul, and Jimmy Casas
(@ToddWhitaker, @Jeff_Zoul, @casas_jimmy)

Excellent leaders and teachers *Know the Way, Show the Way, Go the Way, and Grow Each Day.* Whitaker, Zoul, and Casas share four key behaviors of excellence from educators across the U.S. and motivate to put you on the right path.

Lead Like a PIRATE

Make School Amazing for Your Students and Staff

By Shelley Burgess and Beth Houf
(@Burgess_Shelley, @BethHouf)

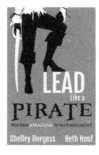

Lead Like a PIRATE maps out character traits necessary to captain a school or district. You'll learn where to find treasure already in your classrooms and schools—and bring out the best in educators. Find encouragement in your relentless quest to make school amazing for everyone!

Teaching Math with Google Apps

50 G Suite Activities

By Alice Keeler and Diana Herrington

(@AliceKeeler, @mathdiana)

Teaching Math with Google Apps meshes the easy student/teacher interaction of Google Apps with G Suite that empowers student creativity and critical thinking. Keeler and Herrington demonstrate fifty ways to bring math classes into the twenty-first century with easy-to-use technology.

Table Talk Math

A Practical Guide for Bringing Math into Everyday Conversations

By John Stevens (@Jstevens009)

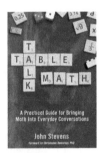

In *Table Talk Math,* John Stevens offers parents—and teachers—ideas for initiating authentic, math-based, everyday conversations that get kids to notice and pique their curiosity about the numbers, patterns, and equations in the world around them.

Shift This!

How to Implement Gradual Change for Massive Impact in Your Classroom

By Joy Kirr (@JoyKirr)

Establishing a student-led culture focused on individual responsibility and personalized learning *is* possible, sustainable, and even easy when it happens little by little. In *Shift This!,* Joy Kirr details gradual shifts in thinking, teaching, and approach for massive impact in your classroom.

Unmapped Potential

An Educator's Guide to Lasting Change

By Julie Hasson and Missy Lennard (@PPrincipals)

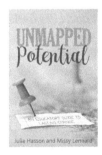

Overwhelmed and overworked? You're not alone, but it can get better. You simply need the right map to guide you from frustrated to fulfilled. *Unmapped Potential* offers advice and practical strategies to forge a unique path to becoming the educator and *person* you want to be.

Shattering the Perfect Teacher Myth

6 Truths That Will Help You THRIVE as an Educator

By Aaron Hogan (@aaron_hogan)

Author and educator Aaron Hogan helps shatter the idyllic "perfect teacher" myth, which erodes self-confidence with unrealistic expectations and sets teachers up for failure. His book equips educators with strategies that help them shift out of survival mode and THRIVE.

Social LEADia

Moving Students from Digital Citizenship to Digital Leadership

By Jennifer Casa-Todd (@JCasaTodd)

A networked society requires students to leverage social media to connect to people, passions, and opportunities to grow and make a difference. *Social LEADia* helps shift focus at school and home from digital citizenship to digital leadership and equip students for the future.

Spark Learning

3 Keys to Embracing the Power of Student Curiosity

By Ramsey Musallam (@ramusallam)

Inspired by his popular TED Talk "3 Rules to Spark Learning," Musallam combines brain science research, proven teaching methods, and his personal story to empower you to improve your students' learning experiences by inspiring inquiry and harnessing its benefits.

Ditch That Homework

Practical Strategies to Help Make Homework Obsolete

By Matt Miller and Alice Keeler (@jmattmiller, @alicekeeler)

In *Ditch That Homework*, Miller and Keeler discuss the pros and cons of homework, why it's assigned, and what life could look like without it. They evaluate research, share parent and teacher insights, then make a convincing case for ditching it for effective and personalized learning methods.

The Four O'Clock Faculty

A Rogue Guide to Revolutionizing Professional Development

By Rich Czyz (@RACzyz)

In *The Four O'Clock Faculty*, Rich identifies ways to make professional learning meaningful, efficient, and, above all, personally relevant. It's a practical guide to revolutionize PD, revealing why some is so awful and what *you* can do to change the model for the betterment of everyone.

Culturize

Every Student. Every Day. Whatever It Takes.

By Jimmy Casas (@casas_jimmy)

Culturize dives into what it takes to cultivate a community of learners who embody innately human traits our world desperately needs—kindness, honesty, and compassion. Casas's stories reveal how "soft skills" can be honed while exceeding academic standards of twenty-first-century learning.

Code Breaker

Increase Creativity, Remix Assessment, and Develop a Class of Coder Ninjas!

By Brian Aspinall (@mraspinall)

You don't have to be a "computer geek" to use coding to turn curriculum expectations into student skills. Use *Code Breaker* to teach students how to identify problems, develop solutions, and use computational thinking to apply and demonstrate learning.

The Wild Card

7 Steps to an Educator's Creative Breakthrough

By Hope and Wade King (@hopekingteach, @wadeking7)

The Kings facilitate a creative breakthrough in the classroom with *The Wild Card*, a step-by-step guide to drawing on your authentic self to deliver your content creatively and be the *wild card* who changes the game for your learners.

Stories from Webb

The Ideas, Passions, and Convictions of a Principal and His School Family

By Todd Nesloney (@TechNinjaTodd)

    Stories from Webb goes right to the heart of education. Told by award-winning principal Todd Nesloney and his dedicated team of staff and teachers, this book reminds you why you became an educator. Relatable stories reinvigorate and may inspire you to tell your own!

The Principled Principal

10 Principles for Leading Exceptional Schools

By Jeffrey Zoul and Anthony McConnell
(@Jeff_Zou, @mcconnellaw)

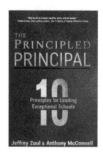

    Zoul and McConnell know from personal experience that the role of school principal is one of the most challenging *and* the most rewarding in education. Using relatable stories and real-life examples, they reveal ten core values that will empower you to work and lead with excellence.

The Limitless School

Creative Ways to Solve the Culture Puzzle

By Abe Hege and Adam Dovico (@abehege, @adamdovico)

    Being intentional about creating a positive culture is imperative for your school's success. This book identifies the nine pillars that support a positive school culture and explains how each stakeholder has a vital role to play in the work of making schools safe, inviting, and dynamic.

Google Apps for Littles

Believe They Can

By Christine Pinto and Alice Keeler
(@PintoBeanz11, @alicekeeler)

    Learn how to tap into students' natural curiosity using technology. Pinto and Keeler share a wealth of innovative ways to integrate digital tools in the primary classroom to make learning engaging and relevant for even the youngest of today's twenty-first-century learners.

Be the One for Kids

You Have the Power to Change the Life of a Child

By Ryan Sheehy (@sheehyrw)

Students need guidance to succeed academically, but they also need our help to survive and thrive in today's turbulent world. They need someone to model the attributes that will help them win not just in school but in life as well. That someone is you.

About the Authors

Together, Rebecca Coda and Rick Jetter are the coauthors of various books, including the highly acclaimed *Escaping the School Leader's Dunk Tank*, also published by Dave Burgess Consulting, Inc. More about this book can be found here:

LeadershipDunkTank.com

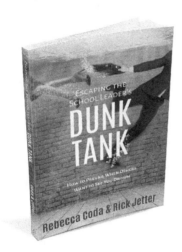

Rebecca Coda, NBCT, is currently the director of K–6 curriculum and instruction in the Cabot Public School District in Arkansas. She has taught grades 4–7 in Florida and Arizona. In the Phoenix metro area she also worked as a K–8 instructional coach, STEM coach, district ELA curriculum specialist, and district technology integration specialist. She is also the founder of the Digital Native Network, which can be found at digitalnativenetwork.net.

You can find out more information about Rebecca here:
RebeccaCoda.com
Twitter, LinkedIn, Facebook, Instagram, and Voxer
@RebeccaCoda

Rick Jetter, Ph.D., is currently a national education consultant, author, speaker, and professional development trainer. He
is the author of *Sutures of the Mind*, *The Isolate*, *Hiring the Best Staff
for Your School*, and *Igniting Wonder, Reflection, and Change in Our
Schools*. He previously worked as a teacher, assistant principal, principal, assistant superintendent, and superintendent of schools.

You can find out more information about Rick here:
RickJetter.com
Twitter, LinkedIn, Facebook, Instagram, and Voxer
@RickJetter